Children from c[...]
families in publi[...]
Northern Ireland

Berni Kelly and Ruth Sinclair

national children's bureau
making a difference

The National Children's Bureau promotes the interests and well-being of all children and young people across every aspect of their lives. NCB advocates the participation of children and young people in all matters affecting them. NCB challenges disadvantage in childhood.

NCB achieves its mission by
- ensuring the views of children and young people are listened to and taken into account at all times
- playing an active role in policy development and advocacy
- undertaking high quality research and work from an evidence based perspective
- promoting multidisciplinary, cross-agency partnerships
- identifying, developing and promoting good practice
- disseminating information to professionals, policy makers, parents and children and young people

NCB has adopted and works within the UN Convention on the Rights of the Child.

Published by the National Children's Bureau, Registered Charity number 258825. 8 Wakley Street, London EC1V 7QE. Tel: 020 7843 6000. Website: www.ncb.org.uk

© National Children's Bureau, 2003
Published 2003

ISBN 1 900990 98 9

British Library Cataloguing in Publication Data
A catalogue record for this book is available from the British Library

All rights reserved. No part of this publication may be reproduced, stored in a retrieval system or transmitted in any form by any person without the written permission of the publisher.

Contents

List of figures — iv
List of tables — v
Acknowledgements — vi

Introduction — 1

1 Mixed needs or forgotten needs? — 7
2 The research study — 25
3 Barriers for cross-community families — 33
4 Children's experiences of being cross-community — 53
5 Social work and other support services for cross-community families — 73
6 Meeting the needs of cross-community children who are looked after — 89
7 Promoting the religious and cultural identity of looked after children — 123
8 Space for everyone: improving services for cross-community families — 161

References — 173

List of figures

Figure 3.1:	Who makes decisions about children's religious upbringing	43
Figure 3.2:	When parents decide about children's religious upbringing	45
Figure 3.3:	Type of school children attend	48
Figure 4.1:	Children's religious identity	53
Figure 4.2:	Children's views on the importance of religion	54
Figure 4.3:	Children's views on positive or negative aspects of being cross-community	58
Figure 4.4:	Religious background of looked after children's friends	62
Figure 4.5:	Importance of religion to other people at social and leisure clubs	67
Figure 4.6:	Children's views on integration	68
Figure 5.1:	Reasons cross-community children are looked after	78
Figure 6.1:	Social workers assume children's religious identity	91
Figure 7.1:	Level of social services priority for promoting children's identity	135

List of tables

Table 2.1: Number of looked after cross-community children identified by McCay and Sinclair in 1999   27
Table 2.2: Numbers and types of respondents from each H&SS Trust Area   28
Table 2.3: Numbers and types of respondents from NIMMA   29

Acknowledgements

Members of the Advisory Group for this research provided valuable support and encouragement throughout this study and helpful comments on earlier drafts of this report. We thank John Pinkerton from the School of Social Work and Marina Monteith from the Institute of Child Care Research at Queens University Belfast, Marion Reynolds from the Social Services Inspectorate, Eamon McTernan from the Western Health and Social Services Board, Colin McKay from Down and Lisburn Health and Social Services Trust, Paul Connolly from the University of Ulster, Goretti Horgan from Save the Children, Michael Neely from the Research and Development Office and Harry Barry from South and East Belfast Health and Social Services Trust. Our thanks are also due to the R&D Office who funded this research.

We wish to thank the R&D Office for funding the research. We also wish to thank the University of Ulster for providing accommodation and support for the research and hosting the launch of this report.

Particular thanks is extended to the children, parents and carers who took time to participate in this research and share their personal experiences with the researcher. We also thank members of NIMMA and social work staff at the five Health and Social Services Trusts who openly and willingly gave their valuable time to participate in this study. Without the cooperation and involvement of these participants it would not have been possible to deliver the compelling messages in this report.

Berni Kelly
Ruth Sinclair
July 2003

Introduction

Northern Ireland was created out of conflict in 1921 and conflict has been present throughout much of its history, particularly with the re-emergence of 'the troubles' in 1968. Today, as much as ever, Northern Ireland is a society characterised by conflict and sectarianism, where division and segregation pervades almost all aspects of children's lives. For example, 95 per cent of children attend schools separated by religion; 80 per cent of public housing is heavily segregated and increasingly children only have friends from the same community background as themselves. There is now a growing body of research that has examined the impact upon children of living through 'the troubles' and in a divided, conflictual society. However, almost all this research has assumed that children are from either the Catholic or Protestant community. There has been very little research on the families that have crossed the divide, or on the children from these cross-community families who have one parent from a Catholic background and one from a Protestant background.

It is this group of children who are the focus of this research. More particularly, it is children from this group who are in public care, being looked after by the Health and Social Services Boards and Trusts. From previous research we know that these children are over-represented in the public care system. However, there is still little evidence of why that might be so or the particular or additional needs that these children may face. That is the purpose of the research reported here.

Rationale for the research

In Northern Ireland, religious and cultural identity is inextricably linked to community segregation and politics (Connolly 1999; Connolly and Maginn 1999). Therefore, religious identity is about more than personal beliefs; it will impact on where one lives, works, attends school and socialises. For children from cross-community backgrounds who cross these boundaries in society, religious identity needs are particularly pertinent. If these cross-community children come into public care, become looked after, then meeting their religious and cultural needs will have an added complexity.

Current legislation, such as the Children (NI) Order 1995, places duties on social services to meet the religious and cultural needs of children and to promote anti-sectarianism in their daily practice. This is particularly relevant to children who come from cross-community backgrounds who may have mixed religious and cultural needs (McCay and Sinclair 1999).

Several studies have indicated that families from cross-community backgrounds have particular needs and that there are inadequacies in current support systems for these families (Robinson 1992; Morgan *et al.* 1996; Wigfall-Williams 2001). Indeed, a previous study by the National Children's Bureau (NCB) found that cross-community children are over-represented in the public care system in Northern Ireland (McCay and Sinclair 1999). This over-representation of cross-community children in public care in Northern Ireland can be compared to children of mixed parentage in England who are also more likely to move into public care. In England, the 'colour-blind' approach to ethnic minorities has been widely rejected. When this experience is applied to the Northern Ireland context, social work approaches that ignore community background and the impact of sectarianism may also need to be questioned. Researchers have repeatedly called for more radical and reflexive social work in Northern Ireland that addresses the impact of sectarianism on everyday practice and the lives of families the service works with (Smyth and Campbell 1996; Diamond and Godfrey 1997; Traynor 1998). However, there is a dearth of knowledge about the challenges social workers face in their efforts to deliver support services to cross-community families in the context of a divided society. McCay and Sinclair (1999) recommended further research to examine the needs and experiences of looked after children who come from cross-community backgrounds.

This study aims to address these gaps in knowledge both by investigating the factors that lead to the over-representation of cross-community children in public care and by examining how their particular needs can best be met by service providers. This is the first study that explores the views of children from cross-community backgrounds, in particular those who are looked after. By interviewing children, parents, carers and social workers it is possible to explore the impact of a cross-community background on children's needs and the effectiveness of services provided to meet their needs.

The findings of this report are relevant to children and young people, their parents or carers, policy makers and practitioners. It holds key messages for the planning and development of services for looked after children from cross-community families, in accordance with current legislative duties in Northern Ireland, and how these can be delivered in an anti-sectarian manner.

Defining identity in Northern Ireland

Children's religious and cultural identities are interwoven into the sectarian and political context of Northern Ireland and its divided communities. It is important, therefore, to define the meaning of the terms sectarianism, culture, community and cross-community identity as they are used throughout this report.

Sectarianism in Northern Ireland is more than a religious struggle. It has a diverse complexity related to history, culture, economy and territory with religious identity used as a 'marker' between two communities (Brewer 1991). This allows people to identify the religious, cultural and political identity of individuals and agencies based on indicators such as names, schools or community areas. This process of assumption helps people to avoid confrontation or embarrassment but can also promote stereotypes and can impact on communication in working relationships. Indeed, practitioners may feel it is necessary to disguise such indicators of their religious, cultural and political identity by adapting or denying details of their own background. Therefore, in recognition of the complex nature of sectarianism in Northern Ireland, it is useful to consider Connolly's (1999, p16) definition of sectarianism:

> Sectarianism ... refers to all of those changing sets of ideas and practices which, whether intentionally or unintentionally, tend to construct and reproduce divisions and/or unequal relationships between ethnically defined Catholics and Protestants.

Although there are many subdivisions within these two broad groups, and there are others who fall outside them altogether, it is the division between Catholics and Protestants that domiantes, and hence is the focus of this study.

Cultural identity is also related to many factors, including shared experiences and histories, ethnic and religious identity, family attitudes and class. As cultural identity is not fixed and is inter-connected with so many other variables it is difficult to provide a conclusive definition of the term. In Northern Ireland, cultural identity is closely connected to religious identity. For example, marching on the Twelfth of July is often associated with Protestantism whereas speaking Gaelic is traditionally affiliated with Catholicism. As the participants in this research demonstrate, religious affiliation is often expressed through participation in cultural activities. Hence, consideration of the religious needs of children must also take account of their cultural needs. Since housing and community areas in Northern Ireland are mostly segregated, children and families usually choose to live in communities that reflect their religious and cultural identity (Holliday 1997). Therefore, addressing the religious and cultural needs of children must include consideration of the communities where children can safely live and socialise.

The complex relationship between religion and community background is illustrated by the 2001 census, as applied to Northern Ireland. Information was asked both about religion and about community background, defined as 'religion or religion brought up in'. Whereas almost 14 percent of the population stated they had no religion, less than 2 per cent failed to identify their community background (NISRA, 2003).

Throughout this report we refer to the term 'cross-community' children. This means a child who has one parent from a Catholic background and the other parent from a Protestant background. In some cases we use the term 'Interchurch' (Robinson 1992). In this report, this term differs from 'cross-community' as it specifically refers to Christians who actively belong to both Catholic and Protestant churches.

Two other terms referred to in the report that require definition are 'key worker' and 'key child'. A key worker is a residential social worker who has been designated to be the principal worker responsible to meet the needs of a particular child living in residential care. The term 'key child' refers to a child living in residential care who has a key worker.

Finally, it is important to emphasise that by highlighting the needs of children from cross-community backgrounds it is not intended that these children should be viewed as problematic and hence pathologised. In NCB's previous study, McCay and Sinclair (1999) noted this would only serve to further reduce the likelihood that services would be developed to meet the needs of these children and their families. Instead, we recognise that these children present a significant challenge to sectarianism – they are living examples of how it is possible to cross religious and cultural divisions in Northern Ireland. Indeed, supporting these children and their families and promoting their diverse religious and cultural identities may be one part of an anti-sectarian strategy for service provision in Northern Ireland (Robinson 1992).

Structure of the report

This report begins with discussion of the current legislation governing childcare services in Northern Ireland in relation to meeting the religious and cultural needs of children within an anti-sectarian and anti-discriminatory framework. A review of existing literature on the needs of cross-community children reveals gaps in knowledge about the experiences and needs of these children and their families.

Next, the report sets out the aims of the study and the qualitative methods employed. Details of sampling methods, the process of gaining access to children and their families and the design of semi-structured interview schedules are provided. This chapter also includes discussion of relevant ethical considerations and the limitations of the research.

The interviews with children, parents, carers and social workers yielded rich qualitative data on supporting cross-community families and the experiences of cross-community children in the community and when they become looked after. This data allows for greater understanding of how support services can progress to best meet the needs of these children and their families. Chapters 3 to 7 present the main findings from the study.

Chapter 3 outlines the experiences of cross-community families and the barriers that they face, including negative attitudes, isolation from informal support networks and sectarianism within the community. Parents must often make difficult decisions about their children's upbringing under pressure from family members and the public and within the constraints of a segregated society. Such findings underline the importance of effective support services for these families.

The next chapter discusses children's experience of being cross-community. This includes children's views on their religious identity and their experience of discrimination. This chapter also explores the impact that living in a segregated society can have on the opportunities these children have to maintain a dual identity and to form relationships with peers from mixed backgrounds in integrated social spaces.

The availability and effectiveness of social work and other support services for cross-community families is discussed in Chapter 5. This includes social workers' views on how they fulfil legal duties that require them to meet religious and cultural needs in the context of a segregated sectarian society. Comments from parents reveal inadequacies in service provision for cross-community families who have weak informal support systems.

In Chapter 6, the focus shifts specifically to cross-community children who are looked after. This includes discussion of the challenges social workers face in recording religious and cultural needs and consulting children and families about religious upbringing. Placement issues for cross-community children and factors influencing family contact are also identified.

Chapter 7 discusses how social workers promote cross-community children's religious and cultural identities. Key factors impacting on the religious upbringing of cross-community children who are looked after are identified. Concerns expressed by carers and social workers reveal the need for further training to ensure that they feel adequately skilled to promote positive identities for looked after children from cross-community backgrounds and to deal with sectarian issues.

The final chapter of this report outlines how findings from this study can inform the development of more effective support services for children from cross-community backgrounds and their families, especially looked after children. This study underlines how these children and their families require neutral spaces to be together and, if they wish, to maintain a dual identity without familial or community pressures. Suggestions are addressed to practitioners and policy makers on how to improve service provision for these children and their families in accordance with current legislative duties.

1. Mixed needs or forgotten needs?

The context for this study is the divided and sectarian nature of life in Northern Ireland. This has a major impact on how children live their lives and how services are provided. The current legislative framework in Northern Ireland could be seen to promote anti-discriminatory and anti-sectarian childcare practice. In addition, social services have a legal obligation to consider children's religious and cultural backgrounds. However, within the context of a sectarian society, how aware are social services and other agencies of the needs of children who come from cross-community backgrounds? Is sufficient attention paid to understanding and addressing the identity needs of these children? Or are their needs ignored or simply forgotten? This chapter discusses the impact of sectarianism on children, the practice of social work in a divided society and the implementation of legislative duties in relation to meeting the needs of cross-community children and their families. Particular attention is paid to research on the experiences of these children and their families and evidence that these children are over-represented in the public care system in Northern Ireland.

Sectarianism and segregation in Northern Ireland

In Northern Ireland, sectarianism is not merely a theological dispute. It is related to community belonging and cultural traditions that are only sometimes linked to the religious beliefs of Catholicism and Protestantism. Connolly (1999) suggested that sectarianism is not only applicable to a minority of extremists but directly influences everyone living and working in Northern Ireland. Thus, sectarianism is apparent at all levels of social, political and economic organisations (Connolly and Maginn 1999).

As a result of sectarianism, Northern Ireland has become a deeply divided society with widespread residential, educational and social segregation. The

Department of Education recently approved the establishment of several new integrated schools in Northern Ireland, thereby demonstrating growing support for the development of the integrated sector. However, integrated education in Northern Ireland still remains small with figures for the 2001–2002 school year showing that there were only 47 integrated schools, providing for less than 5 per cent of the school population (NICIE 2002). Many writers have expressed concern that educational segregation has contributed to divisions in Northern Irish communities by encouraging sectarian defensiveness, fear and suspicion (Fitzduff and Frazer 1986; Wright 1993; Muldoon *et al.* 2000). Similarly, housing areas in Northern Ireland, especially public housing, are mostly segregated. A recent report confirmed that almost 100 per cent of Housing Executive estates in Belfast were segregated (NIHE 1999). Indeed, statistics from the *Northern Ireland Life and Times Survey* in 1999, reveal that almost three quarters of respondents still prefer to live in neighbourhoods with only people from their own community background (Hughes and Donnelly 2001).

This persistent segregation at all levels of Northern Irish society has a strong influence on the continuation of sectarian divisions. Indeed, recent evidence from the *Life and Times Survey* suggests that, despite the 'peace process', division and the desire for segregation has increased in the past two years (Hughes and Donnelly, 2001). Holliday (1997) acknowledged that as a result of such divisions many children do not have opportunities to even meet members of the 'other' community. Shirlow's (1999) survey of almost 5,000 Catholic and Protestant households in housing estates in Belfast, found evidence of increased segregation, sectarianism and bigotry over the past decade, especially among young people. Of the 18 to 25-year-olds surveyed, 68 per cent claimed to never have had a 'meaningful conversation' with anyone from the other community. In all age groups surveyed, almost two thirds had experienced physical or verbal abuse from someone from the other community background since the ceasefires of 1994. Likewise, an NCB study involving 114 young people in Northern Ireland found that almost 70 per cent only had friends from the same community background and almost half of these young people preferred to live in a segregated area (McCole *et al.* 2003). Such segregation can lead to alienation and the development of false stereotypes about the other community and their role in conflict in Northern Ireland (Kelly 2002; McCole *et al.* 2003).

Children's experience of sectarianism

A vast amount of literature has explored the impact of conflict in Northern Ireland over the years (Fraser 1973; Harbison 1983; Cairns 1987, 1996; Byrne 1997; Holliday 1997; Smyth 1998; Smyth and Robinson 2001). From the 1970s onwards more attention was paid to children and young people. However, most of this literature concentrated on the effects of the conflict on children's attitudes and behaviour and usually involved older children in psychological tests of their awareness of symbols, pictures and words (Stringer and Cairns 1983). Such quantitative research examining the impact of the conflict on children and young people has discovered that they are resilient and do not suffer serious psychological problems as a result of conflict (Cairns 1996; Joseph *et al.* 1993; Muldoon *et al.* 2000; Muldoon and Trew 2000).

However, Connolly and Maginn (1999) criticised such quantitative research for applying adult cognitive tests to children without either considering their experiences or exploring how significant children's attitudes were to their changing sense of identity in the context of their lives. The authors argued that previous research was descriptive in nature rather than explanatory and underestimated children's social and cognitive ability to describe and explain their own experiences. Therefore, researchers have begun to adopt qualitative methodological approaches to develop an understanding of children's views of living in a divided society and their subjective experiences of sectarianism. Connolly (1997; 1999) and Connolly *et al.* (2002) provided research evidence that challenged previous assumptions about the inability of younger children to understand values such as mutual respect. Their research suggested that children's cultural identity and attitudes changed over time in different social contexts and emphasised that sectarianism was not confined to individual prejudices but was reproduced through peer relationships and within a range of social, political and economic structures.

Considering reports that children have not suffered major psychological problems alongside findings that children are active interpreters of their experiences emphasises the need for strong family, peer and community support networks so that children can fully understand and appropriately respond to sectarian abuse or political violence. Indeed, Muldoon and Cairns (1999) suggested that children in Northern Ireland continued to cope and adapt successfully because they adopted effective problem-solving mechanisms and were protected by adult care-givers when they had negative experiences of conflict. Likewise, Connolly (1997) recognised the need to actively engage with the children about their anxieties and encourage them to discuss and reflect upon their beliefs and experiences.

Unfortunately, little of this research has considered the experiences of children from cross-community backgrounds. However, research on children in general in Northern Ireland could be considered all the more relevant to the lives of children from cross-community backgrounds who may experience discrimination from both communities and increased isolation amidst widespread segregation in Northern Ireland. Various authors have provided suggestions on how to adopt an anti-sectarian approach or address community relations issues with children and young people in general (Lampen 1995; Community Relations Council 1997; Playboard 1997; NICIE 1998). Connolly (1999) recommended explicit discussion and debate about the meaning and nature of sectarianism and effective strategies for addressing sectarianism. He suggested it is important to recognise that sectarian attitudes are not simply a result of ignorance but are founded on real experiences and anxieties. Therefore, community relations work must be sensitive and take into consideration the broader political and economic environment. There have also been considerable efforts to support anti-sectarian practice in social work (Bagnall *et al.* 1995; CCETSW 1999). However, Geraghty (1999) noted that open discussion about issues related to conflict and sectarian divisions were rare within public organisations in Northern Ireland. She urged governmental agencies to recognise the rights and experiences of children and young people directly and indirectly affected by the conflict, including their experience of community tensions, restrictions of segregated social spaces, disadvantage and discrimination.

The legislative context

The legal framework of Northern Ireland includes legislation that is relevant to the whole United Kingdom as well as that specific to Northern Ireland. With regards to children and their rights, the United Nations Convention on the Rights of the Child (UNCRC) and the European Convention on Human Rights (ECHR) have particular relevance.

The United Nations Convention on the Rights of the Child was ratified by the United Kingdom government in 1991. This Convention is a legally binding international agreement outlining the rights of all children irrespective of class, ethnicity or religion. Articles 12 and 13 promote the development of policies that facilitate the expression of children's views in any decisions made about their lives:

> State parties shall assure to the child who is capable of forming his or her own views the right to express those views freely in all matters affecting the child. (Article 12)

> A child has the right to obtain and make known information and to express his or her views, unless this would violate the rights of others. (Article 13)

In addition, Article 2 specifies that State parties must ensure children are:

> protected against all forms of discrimination or punishment on the basis of the status, activities, expressed opinions, or beliefs of the child's parents, legal guardians, or family members

Article 8 states that State parties must:

> respect the right of the child to preserve his or her identity, including nationality, name and family relations

Article 30 considers children's cultural and linguistic identity:

> In those States in which ethnic, religious or linguistic minorities or persons of indigenous origin exist, a child belonging to such a minority or who is indigenous shall not be denied the right, in community with other members of his or her group, to enjoy his or her own culture, to profess and practise his or her own religion, or to use his or her own language

In addition, Article 31 recognises the rights of children to have equal opportunities to access social, cultural, leisure and recreational activities and Article 14 promotes respect for the children's right to 'freedom of thought, conscience and religion'.

Also relevant to service provision for children and families is the Human Rights Act (1998). The key aspects of this Act are that it allows individuals to claim their rights under the European Convention on Human Rights (ECHR) in courts in Northern Ireland and it ensures legislation and public policy are compatible with the ECHR (Stevens 2000). The ECHR is concerned with liberty, freedom of speech and privacy and recognises the importance of private family life (Levy 2000).

Specific to Northern Ireland, Section 75 of the Northern Ireland Act (1998) also imposes specific duties on public authorities in Northern Ireland. This Section outlines the Statutory Equality Obligations and includes a requirement for public authorities to promote equality of opportunity and good relations in policy and practice between people of different religious belief, political opinion and racial group. Agencies, including the Department of Health, Social Services and Public Safety, must ensure that new and existing policies comply with Section 75 obligations.

The Children (NI) Order 1995 is one of the most important legislative frameworks governing childcare provision in Northern Ireland. This outlines the duties and responsibilities of Health and Social Services Boards and Trusts[1] with regard to the provision of services for children and families. The principles and duties imposed by the Order can be seen as anti-discriminatory and anti-sectarian in intent. Within the Order, specific duties are also included regarding ascertaining the views of children, supporting children and their families and promoting children's religious and cultural identities.

The Order and its accompanying Guidance places emphasis on the need to ascertain the views and wishes of children and their families, especially for children who are looked after (Article 3 (3) (a)). It also imposes duties on Trusts to provide a range of support services to safeguard and promote the welfare of children in need in their area and promote the upbringing of these children by their families (Article 18 and Schedule 2). And in recognition of the importance of family contact in relation to promoting looked after children's self-identity, the Order places a duty on Boards and Trusts in Northern Ireland to:

> endeavour to promote contact between the child and his parents, any person who has parental responsibility, any relative, friend or any person connected to him
> (Article 29 (1))

While for the past century much of the legislation relating to the placement of children in care carried requirements to have due regard to religious persuasion in the placement and upbringing of children, the Order reflected a much broader concern to promote children's self-identify through the fullest consideration of their background. Hence a statutory duty was placed on Boards and Trusts to give 'Due consideration … to a child's religious persuasion, racial origin and cultural and linguistic background' (Article 26 (3) (c)) when making decisions about a looked after child. For example in relation to placements the guidance states:

---

1 The Health and Personal Social Services Order 1994 specifies the delegation of statutory functions between the Boards and the Trusts.

> A child's religious and cultural background and ethnic origins are important factors for consideration in any placement decision. (DHSS 1996, Volume 3, para 2.38)

In addition, reflecting earlier legislation, Article 52 (6) (a) specifies that when a care order is in force, Trusts shall not 'cause the child to be brought up in any religious persuasion other than that in which he would have been brought up if the order had not been made.' Furthermore, Article 28 (1) (e) refers to the need to ensure that the foster carer with whom a child is placed is either of the same religious persuasion as the child or gives an undertaking that the child will be brought up in that religious persuasion.

These requirements to address the religious and cultural needs of children recognise the importance of assessing children's developmental needs in a holistic way. In meeting the statutory duties set out in the Children (NI) Order, Trusts are required to develop assessment tools, such as the Looking after Children Materials (DH 1995; DHSS (NI) 1996). These paperwork tools provide a framework for assessing and planning to meet the needs of each child. Within them the child's developmental needs are expressed along seven dimensions: health, education, identity, emotional and behavioural development, family and social relationships, social presentation and self-care.

Important among these is the concept of identity. A child may have identity needs when they lack a strong sense of self and, thus, an understanding of 'who they are and where they have come from' (Parker *et al.* 1991). Social services have a statutory duty to assess the needs any child might have in respect of identity, including religious and cultural identity and to have regard to these when planning to meet their needs. This duty may be carried out, for example, by encouraging the development of a positive self-image and providing opportunities for children to learn about their family, background and culture.

An underlying theme of all of this legislation is the principle of equality of opportunity with regard to service provision and consideration of the religious and cultural background of children and their families. However, several authors have expressed concerns about the effective implementation of these policies. For example, Titterton (1995) claimed that living in a divided and sectarian society, such as Northern Ireland, directly impacts on children's cultural and linguistic identity and breaches Article 30 of the United Nations Convention on the Rights of the Child. Likewise, Geraghty (1999) criticised the pervasive lack of consultation with children and young people in Northern

Ireland. The current legislative framework encourages optimism for increased participation by children and young people, partnerships with families and recognition of the religious and cultural needs of children and young people. These policies have particular importance for children and families who come from cross-community backgrounds. However, as McCay and Sinclair (1999) noted, translating these principles and statutory duties into practice for children from cross-community backgrounds will be most challenging.

Social work and anti-sectarianism

As can be seen, both current legislation and research findings have posed significant challenges for those working with children, especially in relation to the impact of sectarianism and other forms of discrimination. However, social work practice has traditionally ignored or distanced itself from the effects of sectarianism (Smyth and Campbell 1996). Diamond and Godfrey (1997) argued that social workers often fail to consider the effects of sectarianism on children's identity formation and urged professionals to develop a critical understanding of the diverse needs of children. The experience of growing up and living in a divided society cannot be ignored and the impact of sectarianism is an integral part of wider issues facing families such as, stress, discrimination, homelessness, isolation and marginalisation.

The traditional neutral approach to sectarianism may have been a coping mechanism for practitioners in a tense and sometimes dangerous environment (Glendinning 2001). Social services, like many other service providers in Northern Ireland, could rationalise that neutrality or non-sectarianism was the best approach because it met the needs of service users regardless of their religious or cultural background. Traynor (1998) argued that, since actively promoting anti-sectarianism has the potential to cause discomfort, defensiveness and danger, it is understandable that practitioners compromise professional values with avoidance strategies. Indeed, pressures to conform with the sectarian status quo are equally applicable to researchers who often assume a stance of distant neutrality and objectivity rather than self-reflexivity (Finlay 2001). However, the Children (NI) Order 1995 requires consideration of the religious and cultural needs of children as part of holistic assessments. Effective implementation of the Children (NI) Order requires recognition of the impact of sectarianism on children's lives and the adoption of a clear anti-sectarian strategy.

Actively addressing the impact of sectarianism and societal divisions is also congruent with an ethos of social work that is grounded in anti-discriminatory practice (Dominelli 1988; Thompson 1993; Smyth 1994; Pinkerton 1998; CCETSW 1999). The very difficult, indeed often dangerous, circumstances in which social workers have practiced in Northern Ireland may make their distancing from sectarianism understandable. But social workers cannot avoid sectarianism, as their practice will ultimately either condone or challenge the forces of such discrimination. This suggests that social workers may need to adopt more proactive and critically reflexive approaches to anti-sectarianism that will involve questioning service structures and systems and examining personal prejudices (Traynor 1998; Pinkerton 1998; CCETSW 1999; Pinkerton and Campbell 2002). This may also mean that social workers need advanced training to further develop their skills for working in sensitive and dangerous areas so they can effectively meet the needs of service users in accordance with core social work values and legislative intent (Brewer 1991; Smyth and Campbell 1996; CCETSW 1999). All this presents major challenges for practitioners working with minimal resources and increasing bureaucratic workloads – and may in part explain the pervasive reluctance of social services to face sectarianism in their work with children and families.

Lessons from anti-racist social work

Meeting the religious and cultural needs of children in public care in Northern Ireland has often been compared to that of 'race' and ethnicity among children in care in England, with discussions about the parallels between sectarianism and racism (Brewer 1992). Notwithstanding the added complexity of violent conflict in Northern Ireland, are there any lessons from the development of social work with children from black and minority ethnic groups, especially those of mixed parentage or dual heritage, that are applicable to cross-community children in Northern Ireland?

There is considerable evidence that prior to the Children Act 1989, and arguably since, social work practice with black and minority ethnic group children could be characterised as 'culturally insensitive' or 'colour blind'. Social workers tended to apply their cultural stereotypes of black families, or because of their acknowledged ignorance were too sensitive to intervene in black families, or naively assumed that colour was unimportant as all children are basically the same (MacDonald 1991). Experience has demonstrated that such a 'colour blind' approach did not achieve best outcomes for children from minority ethnic groups, was discriminatory and failed to promote equal opportunities (Barn *et al.* 1997). It was to address these failings that the Children Act 1989 (S. 22 (5) (c)) introduced the specific requirement that local authorities shall take account of a child's ethnicity, which comprises the four elements of race, culture, religion and language. This meant it should no longer be possible to adopt a 'colour blind' approach.

This seems an important message in respect of cross-community children in Northern Ireland, given the findings from the previous NCB study (McCay and Sinclair 1999) which demonstrated a lack of awareness or even denial by social workers and managers of the particular needs of cross-community children.

A common feature of both systems appears to be the poor quality of recording of family backgrounds. While this is mandatory in England as in Northern Ireland, recent evidence highlights continuing concerns (Tunnard, 2002; Sinclair and Hai, 2003).

There may also be parallels to consider in respect of the over representation of cross-community children in the Northern Ireland public care system. There is considerable evidence that indicates that it is children of mixed parentage (or dual heritage) who are most over-represented within the care system in England (Bebbington and Miles 1989; Dutt and Phillips 2000). Explanations for this over-representation include the impact of socio-economic deprivation, family background, poor formal and informal support systems and racism within social services (Alibhai-Brown and Montague 1992; Banks 1992; Farmer and Owen 1995; Okitikpi 1999b).

Phoenix and Owen (1996) commented on how the traditional assumption that children of mixed parentage must accept themselves as black and be treated as black ignored the fact that many children and young people of mixed parentage experienced discrimination because they had a mixed background as well as discrimination from black and white people based on assumptions they were not black or white. In the Northern Irish context, such discrimination was recently reflected in NCB's study of young people's views on addressing anti-sectarianism, which found a quarter of respondents would not marry someone from the other community background because of expected negative attitudes from family members and the community towards mixed marriages (McCole *et al.* 2003).

Projecting assumptions that children of mixed parentage should adopt one cultural identity increases the likelihood they will experience uncertainty about who they are and where they belong and so fails to understand the social realities of children who have mixed backgrounds. Researchers have emphasised the shifting nature of negotiation between multiple identities by children from mixed parentage at different times and in various contexts (Root 1996; Sinclair and Hai 2003). The fluid identities of children from mixed parentage that adjust to societal and environmental contexts illustrates they are not passive victims caught in the middle with poor low self-esteem. Rather, they have a greater awareness of cultural differences and similarities and a clear view of their identity within that continuum (Troyna and Hatcher 1992; Tizard and Phoenix 1993). Tizard and Phoenix (1993) advocated that agencies and professionals should allow space for self-identification and multiple cultural identities. Children who can participate in open dialogue with their family and others about their mixed identity are more likely to identify with both backgrounds and recognise the advantages and disadvantages associated with their dual heritage (Small 1986; Okitikpi 1999a; Prevatt Goldstein 1999). These studies have challenged pathological views of children of mixed parentage (Tizard and Phoenix 1993; Katz 1996; Okitikpi 1999b). Indeed, they illustrate that children from mixed parentage pose a major ideological challenge to society as they exert pressure for a reconsideration of the relationship between two cultures and whether or not the future requires religious or cultural boundaries (Spencer 1997).

Therefore, alongside the need for social workers to more effectively address sectarianism there is also an imperative to celebrate dual heritage and re-evaluate approaches towards working with children from cross-community backgrounds and their families. Addressing the needs of these children and their families is all the more crucial in the context of Northern Ireland where professionals and people in general still struggle to combat sectarianism. Social workers will need to avoid simply labelling children as of one or other culture if they are to fulfil the social work ethos of understanding difference, working with diversity and upholding children's interests as paramount. Research and literature in England on children of mixed parentage urges social workers to increase their awareness of the additional pressures facing these children and their families and promote their dual cultural heritage. Just as the traditional 'colour-blind' approach in England has been rejected, lack of awareness of the impact of community backgrounds of children in Northern Ireland also fails to promote positive self-identity for children from cross-community backgrounds (Smyth and Campbell 1996; McCay and Sinclair 1999). Indeed, this may be more pertinent in the Northern Irish context where religious identity acts as such a strong marker for community or political affiliation in a divided society.

Research on cross-community families

Given the segregated nature of Northern Irish society it is hardly surprising that those in cross-community relationships may feel vulnerable. However, despite the wide range of research on Northern Irish society and sectarianism, few studies have examined the experiences of those families who actually cross cultural and community boundaries.

The *Northern Ireland Life and Times Survey* (1998) found that only 16 per cent of those interviewed felt that most people in Northern Ireland would 'mind a lot' if a close relative married someone of a different religion (Wigfall-Williams and Robinson 2001). Additionally, this survey revealed that support among both Protestant and Catholic communities for integrated education has increased. However, these authors noted that despite these positive results, less than 10 per cent of marriages are cross-community and more than a quarter of respondents would mind an inter-religious marriage within their own family.

Negative attitudes towards mixed marriages were evident in McFarlane's (1979) analysis of gossip in one village in Northern Ireland. These relationships were frowned upon and deemed to bring shame upon one's family. At institutional and structural levels, negative attitudes towards cross-community relationships are also evident. For example, the rules of the Orange Order do not permit membership to those who are married to a Catholic; and churches, especially the Catholic church, have actively discouraged cross-community relationships. Lee (1994) also acknowledged that in Northern Irish society cross-community relationships were mostly socially unacceptable:

> interreligious marriage in NI is likely to be statistically deviant, interactionally difficult and in the eyes of many morally illegitimate (p31)

Drawing on evidence from a later study, Morgan *et al.* (1996) also recommended that churches should develop support for mixed marriage families and provide clearer information to the public about the position of the church. These authors also noted the pressures on cross-community couples because of the segregated nature of public housing in Northern Ireland. Couples were usually forced to make a decision about which community they could live in and often moved away from segregated areas where they had family support networks. The researchers suggest that agencies, such as social services and the Housing Executive, should consider the needs of these families. This was also supported by Glendinning (2001) who pointed to the increasing use of flags and emblems to designate community territories that has the effect of reducing neutral or shared spaces. He urged agencies to take action to protect areas that are mixed and reclaim segregated areas.

Robinson (1992) conducted interviews with people in cross-community marriages in Northern Ireland and although this sample was over-representative of those with third level education, the findings are still important. The author found that it was difficult for these couples to get married and they had to make complex decisions about where to marry, live and how to raise children. Robinson found the reaction from churches was mostly negative and unsympathetic, with some ministers or priests refusing to provide services. A minority of families had sought to ensure their children maintained links with both churches instead of choosing one. While this was seen as the most constructive and innovative option, it was also the most difficult and demanding. Families in this study generally preferred sending their children to an integrated school, however this was not always possible. As a consequence, people were unhappy when their children developed bigoted opinions because of outside influences. Safety was a major issue for couples who lived in segregated areas or those who were members of the security forces.

Overall, most couples in Robinson's study felt their marriage was stronger because they had overcome multiple difficulties related to their cross-community background. However, the majority of interviewees suggested couples entering into or living in a mixed marriage should have access to more help and support. Furthermore, findings from this study indicated that cross-community families must avoid two extremes: pretending their family was not different which only ignored possible disagreements or exaggerating their differences until they caused conflict.

In a more recent study, Wigfall-Williams (2001) explored the factors impacting on cross-community marriages and drew similar conclusions. Given the extent of negative public attitudes towards cross-community relationships, she expressed concern about the elusive nature of avenues for support and affirmation for these couples. Northern Ireland Mixed Marriage Association (NIMMA) did provide such support but operated under a small budget, and perhaps due to concerns about confidentiality and safety, its existence was only known to a small part of the community. She also recommended that ministers and priests should provide more support, advice and guidance for cross-community couples rather than discouraging such relationships with elaborate bureaucratic procedures. Overall, this research found that families were further isolated and marginalised by the agencies supposed to offer support.

Most of these studies on cross-community relationships have focused on adults who were and remained married with little attention paid to families experiencing significant difficulties or to the experiences of children. Robinson (1992) recognised that children from cross-community backgrounds are influenced by their family upbringing and schools or other institutions that align children with the dominant norm. Additionally, both Robinson (1992) and Morgan *et al.* (1996) emphasised the need to promote a positive identity for cross-community children that embraces both sides of their background. However, none of these studies examined children's perspectives or explored in detail parental perceptions of their child's developing identity. Indeed, Robinson (1992) concluded:

> The issue of identity is a complex one and one that could not be fully addressed in this study but many couples did worry about their own identity and that of their children. (p40)

The needs of children from cross-community families

Given that some cross-community families report difficulties in helping their children develop a positive self-image, it seems that identity is a key issue for these children. Indeed, the Northern Ireland Social Services Inspectorate also recognised the importance of identity for all children in establishing its Standards for providing residential or foster services to children who are looked after (SSI(NI) 1994, 1995).

As noted earlier, identity is now recognised as one of the seven dimensions of the developmental needs of children. Promoting a positive self-identity for children requires understanding of a child's family background, including their religion and culture, and consideration of the child's group identification, that is, their place in society (Dutt and Phillips 2000). This is all the more relevant when children come from cross-community backgrounds who may wish to develop a bi-cultural identity.

Developing self-identity is particularly important for children who are separated from their family and live in public care. Thoburn (1994) suggested that essential components of promoting positive self-identity for these children are providing knowledge about children's birth families and maintaining appropriate contact with significant people from the past. Likewise, other authors have emphasised the importance of maintaining children's contact with cultural and familial support networks in their own communities (Masson 1997; Gilligan 2000). V contact with birth families is not possible, Thoburn (1994) suggests that the promotion of self-identity requires skilled social work intervention alongside continued contact with the child's community and culture.

Clearly identity formation is complex and dynamic. It will obviously have many dimensions including class, gender and ethnicity. However in the context of Northern Ireland, religion, culture or community background are perhaps most dominant. So identity is likely to be problematic, especially for children from cross-community backgrounds who live away from their birth families. Research suggests that there is a greater likelihood that those children will encounter problems in identity formation and that there is a general lack of clarity about how to assist these children to develop a positive self-concept within a divided society (Robinson 1992; Morgan *et al* 1996; Leitch and Kilpatrick 1999; McCay and Sinclair 1999). In general, methods for promoting self-identity, positive community relations and addressing sectarianism have been outlined in previous literature (Morrow and Wilson 1996; Fairmichael 1997; Playboard 1997; Community Relations Council 1997; Connolly 1999). However, gaps in the literature have left some questions unanswered. How aware are social workers of the particular needs and experiences of children from cross-community families? Given the traditional neutral stance of social services towards sectarianism perhaps the religious and cultural needs of cross-community children have been ignored. Two studies conducted by the NCB in Northern Ireland began to address some of these questions: an investigation into planning for children in care and one into cross-community children in public care (Horgan and Sinclair 1997; McCay and Sinclair 1999).

Horgan and Sinclair's (1997) study on planning for children in care in Northern Ireland found that consultation with families was viewed as a technical activity that alienated some parents and young people. They also reported difficulty in finding information on case files about the community background of children and their families and, in particular, cross-community backgrounds. Additionally, there was evidence that some social workers guessed or assumed the religion or community background of children. The practice of stereotyping or making assumptions about religious identity is in stark contrast to the principles of consultation and anti-sectarian practice within current legislation (Diamond and Godfrey 1997). As we have noted earlier, religious identity in Northern Ireland is complex as it is inextricably linked to culture and politics.

Horgan and Sinclair (1997) stated:

> The particular cultural issues in NI around the development of a positive identity for all children in care have yet to be addressed. (p51)

NCB's second study on cross-community children in public care explored this matter further (McCay and Sinclair 1999). This prevalence study was based on a random sample of children that was representative of one in five of the looked after population across Northern Ireland and proportionate to the numbers looked after by each Health and Social Services Trust. Findings confirmed the over-representation of children from cross-community families within the public care population in Northern Ireland. At least 17.3 per cent of the sample had parents from different backgrounds (this only includes those where it was possible to positively identify the community background of both the mother and father). This compared to 5.6 per cent of cross-community relationships in the population as a whole (NISRA 1997).

Through examination of case files, this study also discovered that the quality and accessibility of information on case files was extremely inconsistent, especially in respect of information on the community or religious background of children and their families. For example, for more than half of all cases the child's religion, parents' religion and information about siblings was either not on file or was incomplete. While managers expected social workers to directly consult parents about their religious background, social workers frequently assumed the religious background of families. Despite the evidence of missing data on files, staff were optimistic that records were accurate. Most surprisingly, despite the over-representation of cross-community children in public care, no case files recorded a child's mixed background. In all such cases they were designated to a specific religious identity.

Generally, Board and Trust staff involved in this study did not view children from cross-community backgrounds as having particular needs. The possibility that these children may be over-represented had not been considered. McCay and Sinclair (1999) also found that staff usually interpreted their legal responsibility to consider a child's background only in terms of practising religion and not cultural or community background, with little acknowledgement of the complex experiences impacting on the identity needs of cross-community children.

Despite the lack of information on the religious upbringing of siblings, initial indications showed it was likely that they could have a different religious identity. Breakdown of family relationships was a major theme in reasons why children became looked after; 40 per cent of cross-community couples had separated by the time their child became looked after compared to 31 per cent of couples from the same religious identity. Occasional references to mixed relationships on case files reported stress on relationships related to family disapproval and inadequate informal support systems. The authors recommended that further research was required to explore whether these strains increased the likelihood of relationship breakdown resulting in children from these families becoming looked after.

McCay and Sinclair's (1999) study concluded that more in-depth research on the developmental needs of children from cross-community families was required. Such research may help to explain the problems that lead to the over-representation of these children in public care and explore how social services can more effectively address the issues facing these particular children and their families. The Children (NI) Order imposes specific requirements to consider religious and cultural upbringing as part of childcare practice. Legal responsibilities to gather information, work in partnership with families, consider children's religious and cultural needs and take account of children's views have an added complexity for children from cross-community backgrounds. In these situations, making plans to support a child's identity becomes particularly pertinent. However, research indicates these duties are not being adequately applied to the needs of children from cross-community backgrounds.

Summary

Children in Northern Ireland live in a divided sectarian society. While this impacts on the lives of all children, it poses particular difficulties for children from cross-community backgrounds. Current legislation such as the Children (NI) Order 1995 is founded on anti-discriminatory and anti-sectarian principles and imposes legal duties to consider the religious and cultural backgrounds of children. However, researchers have questioned the extent to which social services have successfully addressed the impact of sectarianism on the lives of children and families and on their daily practice. Avoidance of religious and sectarian issues has a direct effect on practitioners' ability to recognise the manifestation of religious and cultural identity – and thus to meet the needs of children, in accordance with current legal obligations. Research on mixed parentage and the inappropriateness of 'colour-blindness' in England may have some relevance to the situation of children from cross-community families living in Northern Ireland. Several studies have already reported that these families have specific needs and recommended that social workers address those needs in their assessment and planning of services. Furthermore, McCay and Sinclair (1999) have provided evidence that, similar to children of mixed parentage in England, children from cross-community families are over-represented in public care in Northern Ireland. Therefore, it is necessary to explore the reasons for this over-representation, examine the needs of these children and parents and investigate how well social services are meeting these children's needs when they become looked after.

2. The research study

This chapter describes the research study. It sets out the aims of the research and discusses the methodological approach which was adopted. It includes details of the design of research and the process of gaining access to respondents. The sampling method is also outlined, and information provided on the number and type of respondents involved in the study.

Research design

The previous chapter reported on an earlier quantitative study which demonstrated clearly that children from cross-community families were over-represented in public care in Northern Ireland. The purpose of this study is to understand more fully why this is the case. The main aims of the study were to:

- explore the issues children from cross-community relationships who are in need and their families are likely to experience

- identify the particular issues experienced by children from cross-community relationships who are looked after

- identify the key factors that may contribute to children from cross-community families becoming looked after

- examine how the particular needs of looked after cross-community children are, or could be, met in accordance with the requirements of Article 26 (3) (c) of the Children (NI) Order.

To address these aims, this study adopted a qualitative research design involving respondents in individual or group interviews. Aside from interviews, case files for looked after children were also read to collect background information before their interview, such as current placement, contact with family and current legal status. This helped the researcher to refocus interview questions appropriately and sensitively to match the experiences of individual children.

As a core element of the study was to develop understanding of the needs and experiences of looked after children from cross-community families, a purposive sampling strategy was employed. Children were sampled from three different settings in order to ensure data was collected from children with a range of experiences. Since the main focus of the study was children who were looked after it was essential to include these children as the most substantial proportion of the sample. However, it was also important to include children who were in contact with social services but had not yet reached the looked after system. This would provide information on the range of support systems available for families who are experiencing problems and the types of support that might prevent children from becoming looked after. Therefore, a sample of children who were classified by social services as being 'in need' under the Children (NI) Order 1995 were included. These families were usually in contact with social services either because of child protection concerns or to receive family support services such as respite care. These two sets of children were accessed through Health and Social Services Trusts (HSSTs) from across Northern Ireland. Finally, it was also deemed useful to involve cross-community children who were living at home and did not have any contact with social services. This would provide information on the general experience of cross-community families and allow for comparison between these children and those subject to social services intervention. A sample of these children was accessed through the Northern Ireland Mixed Marriage Association (NIMMA). NIMMA is a small voluntary organisation that provides information and support for couples in mixed relationships and their children. For further information about NIMMA see their website www.nimma.org.uk.

Because the children in these three groups will have had different experiences, especially concerning family life, the findings from each group are reported separately throughout this report.

Looked after children and children in need

To increase the likelihood of accessing sufficient numbers of looked after children and children in need for the sample it was necessary to involve the five Trusts who had the highest prevalence of cross-community children as recorded in our previous study (McCay and Sinclair 1999). One of these Trusts, Down and

Lisburn, was used for the pilot study and the other four for the main study: Foyle, Homefirst, South and East Belfast and Sperrin Lakeland HSST. These Trusts cover both rural and urban areas and reflect a range of social and environmental characteristics from across Northern Ireland. Data collected for the pilot study was also included in the findings as no significant changes were made to the interview approach following the pilot and emergent themes from the pilot were similar to those identified from interviews in the other four Trusts.

Table 2.1 illustrates the number of looked after children from the one in five sample who were identified in the previous study to be from cross-community families (McCay and Sinclair 1999). This provided the initial sampling frame for the study.

Table 2.1 Number of looked after cross-community children identified by McCay and Sinclair in 1999

Trust	Number of cross-community children
Down & Lisburn	6
Foyle	9
Homefirst	18
South & East Belfast	8
Sperrin/Lakeland	8

Source: McCay and Sinclair (1999, p20)

As a much higher proportion of cross-community children lived in Homefirst Trust it was decided that more children would be selected from this Trust than the other three. Hence, the sample was to comprise six children from each of Down & Lisburn, Foyle and Sperrin/Lakeland Trusts, five children from South and East Belfast Trust and twelve children from Homefirst Trust.

To identify these children, the researcher started from the details available from the previous study of cross-community children who were looked after in each Trust. The researcher checked if these children were still looked after and within the age range of six to 21 years. This age range was based on the fact that children below six may not be able to articulate a range of experiences of religious or cultural issues and young people up to age 21 would have valuable information about their experiences and could still be receiving support from social services. Children who met all of these criteria were included in the sample frame. In Trusts where there were not sufficient numbers of children available to participate in the study based on these original details, social workers were asked to identify other children who met the criteria until the number of children required for the desired sample size was identified. Successful efforts were made to purposefully select looked after children to include a range of characteristics such as legal status, type of placement and contact with family. The final sample of looked after children included seven sets of siblings. This meant that for a total of 17 children involved in this study some of their siblings were also interviewed. This added to the depth of data collected for these family cases.

For each looked after child involved in the study, their field social worker, birth parent and foster carer or residential key worker were also invited to participate in an interview. Additionally, the principal social worker in each Trust was interviewed about policy issues. This helped to build a full picture of the experiences of these children as well as developing knowledge of the challenges for social workers seeking to meet their needs.

Table 2.2 shows the total numbers of each set of respondents that were interviewed from each Trust area.

Table 2.2 Numbers and types of respondents from each H&SS Trust Area

Trust	Parent of child in need	Children in need	Looked after children	Parent of looked after child	Foster carer	Residential social worker	Field social worker	Principal social worker
Foyle	1	2	6	3	4	1	4	1
Sperrin/ Lakeland	1	1	6	3	3	1	4	1
Homefirst	5	4	12	4	4	5	4	1
South & East Belfast			4	1	1	2	5	1
Down & Lisburn	1	2	6	1	3	1	4	1
Total	8	9	34	12	15	10	21	5

Children and parents in contact with NIMMA

Table 2.3 identifies the numbers of children and parents in contact with NIMMA who were involved in this study. All of these children lived at home with their parents and none of them had contact with social services. Two of these parents had children who were over 21 years old and no longer lived at home. These parents were still interviewed because they had had valuable experience both as parents of cross-community children and as volunteers with NIMMA. A further two parents were also volunteers with NIMMA. Their children were also included in the sample because they were under 21 years old.

Table 2.3 Numbers and types of respondents from NIMMA*

Parents	6
Children	5
Focus group	1 group of 6 children

*Northern Ireland Mixed Marriage Association

Aside from individual interviews with children and parents, the researcher also had an opportunity to conduct a focus group with children at NIMMA's annual conference. This focus group included six children aged between ten and 15 years, who were from cross-community families and were members of NIMMA. This was a useful opportunity to collect data on the shared experiences of children from cross-community relationships in a group setting.

Gaining access and consent

Seeking consent for looked after children to participate in the study involved making a series of contacts. First, social workers forwarded a letter to birth parents, where possible, to inform them about the study and seek their consent. Birth parents were offered two weeks to contact their social worker if they did not wish for themselves or their child to participate. If parents did not respond or responded positively then letters were then sent to foster carers to inform them about the project and seek consent to approach the child and to interview the carer. Where birth parents were not contactable, significant external family members, foster carers or key workers were consulted. Finally, on visits to children consent was gained directly from them and this was continually checked throughout the interview process. Similarly, for children in need, social workers forwarded consent letters to parents and subsequently consent was negotiated with children directly. Families in contact with NIMMA volunteered their willingness to participate in the study at their annual conference.

Confirming the confidential nature of the research process was very important for respondents. It was recognised that some questions could seem intrusive or personal and had to be explained, carefully worded and relevantly placed within the interview. This was particularly pertinent for birth parents since some did not have contact with their children and were reluctant to revisit negative experiences related to their children becoming looked after. Gaining access to these parents was often challenging, either because social workers did not have their current contact details or parents were unwilling to participate. Likewise, accessing children in need and their parents was very difficult and in one Trust area proved impossible. This was because social workers did not routinely record the religious background of children in need and, therefore, could not easily identify children from cross-community relationships. Additionally, when families were identifiable they were often suspicious of requests from social workers about their involvement in this study as they were often under investigation by social services because of childcare-related issues. Given this situation, it is understandable that some families preferred not to participate.

These access issues meant the researcher had to spend more time than anticipated identifying additional possible research participants and, in South and East Belfast HSST it restricted the number of families interviewed. However, this qualitative study sought in-depth data on experiences and explanations rather than generalisable conclusions based on representative samples. Interviewing fewer families than intended for the sample of children in need did not affect the overall quality of the data collected.

Constructing interview questions

Semi-structured interviewing was the most appropriate method of data collection as it allowed more opportunity to provide deeper insights into the views and experiences of families and professionals. Within this approach, questions were defined but could be adapted as individual respondents revealed particular feelings and experiences (Rubin and Rubin 1995; Hill 1997). Separate, semi-structured schedules were devised for interviewing children, parents, carers and social workers, each covering similar themes and offering the respondents the opportunity to add other information.

The possible unfamiliarity of the interview process and the fact this was the first time some children had been asked about their experiences of being cross-community meant the approach for interviews with children required flexible and diverse question formats. For this reason, drawing on the work of other researchers who have employed such creative methods in their research with children, children were asked questions that invited a range of answering styles including verbal, written and pictorial answers (McAuley 1996; Stalker 1998; Bricher 1999; Kelly *et al.* 2000). For example, on occasions children were shown questions using illustrated sentence completion exercises or projective techniques.

Analytical process

All interviews were tape-recorded with the respondents' consent and later transcribed. Qualitative data collected from each respondent was thematically analysed inductively. The key themes from these findings are presented in the next four chapters. Themes emerging from each set of respondents were compared to check for any divergent or common experiences. This was particularly relevant when examining data collected from looked after children in comparison to information from children in need and children from NIMMA, as they had significantly different experiences. These comparisons are discussed throughout the findings presented in upcoming chapters.

Summary

A qualitative methodological approach was adopted for this study to explore the needs and experiences of cross-community children and their families in a range of settings. Data was collected from children and the key people in children's lives including parents, carers and professionals. In this way it was possible to build a reliable and comprehensive view of each child's circumstances and experiences. Practical and ethical issues impacted on the research process. However, sufficient numbers of children, families and professionals from each set of respondents were involved in the study to provide valuable information to fulfil the original aims and objectives of the study.

3. Barriers for cross-community families

This chapter, and the next four chapters, contain the findings from the study presented under key themes and illustrated by quotations from those interviewed. We start, in this chapter, with the experiences of cross-community families and examine the attitudes they encountered from family and friends and the wider community at different stages or when key decisions had to be made: when the relationship was first known, at marriage, choosing the religious identity for themselves and their children, deciding where to live, and selecting their children's school. The impact of the attitudes of others and levels of formal and informal support are explored.

Reactions from family

Almost all of the parents interviewed (22 out of 26) experienced problems with family reactions to their cross-community relationship. Interestingly, only parents of children looked after experienced problems from both families, indicating that these families have the lowest levels of informal support systems.

Problems parents experienced were related to family rejection of one or both parents solely on the basis of their religious background. The quotations below demonstrate the experiences of families who had such negative reactions:

> My mother was the worst. She just thought 'You've disgraced the family name.' Everyone else took it well … I fell pregnant and I didn't want to face my mum so we went to Scotland. We set up home there but my husband hated his job so we returned. Then we had a problem with my husband's father. We stayed at his home when we returned to face the music. One day I was feeding the oldest and he said 'No Orange bastard is welcome in this home. She's not welcome or that child's not welcome.' After that I left immediately.
> *(Mother of looked after child).*

> Well I didn't tell my family very early on ... and when I did tell them about it my father told me that I wasn't any longer welcome in the house. I took just visiting once a week when he wasn't about ... I think the most difficult for my mother was that we weren't married legally in the eyes of the church, you know ... she didn't agree with it and a couple of days before I got married she shut me out.
> **(Mother, NIMMA)**

Several parents from broken cross-community relationships re-married into another cross-community relationship. These parents had experienced negative reactions to their relationships on both occasions. Three parents were in a relationship with someone who previously served in the British Army in Northern Ireland. These parents were even more dislocated from their families because they had to move to non-threatening areas and cease contact with their family for safety reasons:

> His father was a soldier and I was from [Republican area] so they took a lot of grief at the beginning. I moved just for my safety but it was for the safety of my family, my mother and father. I stopped speaking to my family for about two and a half years after I met him because they were more afraid of people getting the information about him and my mum, you know, the whole sectarian thing. I couldn't handle it.
> **(Mother of looked after child)**

Parents involved in this study who had not experienced difficulties with family reactions to their cross-community relationship felt this was because: one partner changed their religious identity; families understood it was the couple's own choice; or families were happy when they got to know the individual rather than making negative assumptions about them based on their religious identity.

Decreased informal family support

Overall, half of the parents from across the sample felt that relationships with their families changed when they developed a cross-community relationship. Those who felt relationships did not change explained their family maintained contact despite their disapproval or were not concerned about their partner's religious background. Those who felt their family relationships did change described their experience of rejection:

> My family disowned me for three years. It was very hard. It took forever to get them back …
> *(Mother of looked after child)*

> They disowned me … I have no contact with them at all even though they live in the same village.
> *(Father of child in need)*

Half of parents from NIMMA and half of parents of children in need felt that support from their families lessened as a result of their cross-community relationship. For parents of looked after children the proportion was slightly higher, with seven out of 12 parents feeling informal family support lessened.

Being rejected by families weakened parents' informal support networks and increased the isolation that cross-community families already experienced:

> My husband's family weren't supportive at all. My family made me more independent so I wouldn't ask for anything. I was left thinking I had made my bed so now I had to lie in it.
> *(Mother of looked after child)*

The absence of informal family support and coping with strained family relationships left families feeling isolated and stressed. Indeed, even some parents who felt support from their family did not lessen admitted there were still tensions within family relationships:

> No, not support but you know, always hassling with the family.
> *(Mother, NIMMA)*

Families who still had strong support from their family described how essential this was for their cross-community family.

> Well I was pregnant when we got married and I think the family were pleased for both of us but I think really because all of what we are, we're being mixed that's very important because, you know, I do really very much think the mix can contribute to a break up. There is no doubt. A lot of people deny it but it definitely can.
> *(Mother, NIMMA)*

Marriage

The majority of all the parents involved in this study had married. However, eight out of the 34 parents of looked after children had not married. Six of these parents had lived with their partner but had also separated. At the time of the study, all of the parents from NIMMA were still married and only one out of the six married parents of children in need had separated. However, only one couple from the 26 married parents of looked after children were still together. This again highlights the differences in the three groups involved in the study.

Parents explained that the process of getting married was difficult for cross-community couples. Some parents had to make decisions about the upbringing of their children and changing their own religious identity in order to get married due to pressures from their families or the church.

> I was Protestant but I turned to be Catholic. I had to be baptised and do Holy Communion and Confirmation and weeks of work with the priest – it was like going to school. The priest was Irish and he was set in his ways. As far as he was concerned nobody in the parish could be Protestant and my husband followed him. He used the children as a weapon against me because he knew I wanted to take part. He said I wouldn't be able to take part in the upbringing of the children if I wasn't Catholic. You need to be Catholic for the children to be Catholic.
> ***(Mother of looked after child)***

> We got married in a Catholic chapel and mum liked that. [husband] wasn't that happy about it but he had to do it. We asked the minister and he was very nice but it's their rule that you can't have a mixed marriage and with the Catholic church the children have to be Catholic.
> ***(Mother of child in need)***

Most parents found they had to negotiate between the wishes and feelings of both families in order to avoid offending relatives.

> It was in the Catholic Church. My Methodist minister was there. Him being there was more for my family than it was for me. We organised a smaller wedding, deliberately.

> I suppose it was to make it easier in the sense that neither family would have to be exposed to too many of the other family but also there was a sense that it wasn't too public by inviting all sorts of other relatives who knew so we went round relatives and told them openly ... I do know that some thought don't worry about it he will be a convert in a few years!
> *(Father, NIMMA)*

> The only sort of stress I think which we probably alluded to was trying to please both parents, both sets of families, but realising twenty years later that whatever you did it didn't matter! Sometimes I wonder why you bother ... It still annoys me because I like to please and that creates a lot of tensions and stress.
> *(Mother, NIMMA)*

Parents who had separated or divorced felt their relationships ended for a range of reasons including problems related to alcohol addiction, domestic violence, physical abuse or infidelity. However, many parents also recognised the impact of stressors on cross-community relationships. These included disagreements about children's religious upbringing; conflict with external family members; arguments about religion or politics; and pressures related to living in segregated society, such as intimidation. The quotations below illustrate how these stressors impacted on the daily lives of cross-community families:

> It created an awful lot of problems. His family wouldn't have accepted a Protestant. There were rows and I was called names. Our views were totally different like if something was on the TV about killing soldiers. I learnt to shut my mouth because I couldn't voice an opinion.
> *(Mother of looked after child)*

> My first husband was the opposite. He was very staunch. I wanted [child] baptised and he said no but I did it anyway and I am glad I did now. He wasn't there. He didn't even know anything about it because I did it behind his back.
> *(Mother of looked after child)*

> There was rows about rearing the children Catholic – that was [husband's] idea and I wasn't too happy about it. It just caused rows.
> *(Mother of looked after child)*

> It causes arguments and being burnt out and targeted by the paramilitaries – leaves you wrecked.
> *(Mother of Child in Need)*

> It's certainly the rowing and I do feel it's probably mostly that which caused the friction with ourselves when we were rearing the children, also I suppose the politics, I would have been brought up with very strong Irish identity and he would be more British sympathies … you do have a good healthy or unhealthy bit of sectarianism, you can't help it but I think the religion that would probably be the biggest difficulty for us.
> *(Mother, NIMMA)*

On the other hand, some parents felt that being in a cross-community relationship made their marriage stronger:

> We just slag each other about it. It actually brings you closer because you have to hang with one another and it helps see both sides clearer.
> *(Mother of child in need)*

> I think it enhances the relationship and makes it more interesting.
> *(Mother, NIMMA)*

These findings show that being in a cross-community relationship has both the potential to create serious problems for families and, conversely to enrich their relationships. It seems that how families cope with the stresses of being cross-community has an important impact on the maintenance of strong family relationships. Overcoming such stressors, however, was all the more difficult with the absence of approval and support from family members.

Changing religious identities

None of the parents from NIMMA or parents of children in need changed their religion as a result of being in a cross-community relationship. Although none of the fathers of looked after children had changed their religion, three mothers had. Two Protestant mothers became Catholic and one Catholic mother became Protestant. Interestingly, another Protestant mother and Protestant father felt that, although they had not changed their religion they did practise Catholicism because they attended Catholic services and reared their children as Catholic.

Mothers who changed their religious identity described still feeling like an outsider in the community they had joined. In one case, a parent who came from a cross-community background was baptised Protestant but then married a Catholic and became Catholic herself. She described never being accepted as a 'real' Catholic. Later she separated from her husband and formed a new relationship with a Protestant partner. Interestingly, she then experienced the same difficulties with his family who did not accept her because they viewed her as Catholic since she had married a Catholic and reared her children as Catholic. She described feeling lost in her identity between the two communities and never being accepted wholly into either:

> When I got married I had to have Catholic instruction because I wanted one religion. I knew the problems of having two religions. I didn't want a mixed marriage. It was too confusing for everybody. I would've been a Protestant wife in a very Republican area but it was okay because I turned. But his name is a label now hanging round our necks. He was a strict Catholic … but it was made obvious to me even when he was joking that he felt I didn't know enough about it to talk about it. For him I wasn't a real Catholic like he was. He would say 'sure what do you know?'… Now I'm engaged to a fella … He's Presbyterian. His family are very loyal and bitter and his mum doesn't like me. His first wife was Protestant and they see me as Catholic because of who I was married to and my kids. It's very hard to go back to your original religion when you have changed or married into another … I'm in between two worlds myself between Catholic and Protestant although I'm more Catholic I see myself as Protestant but I'm not part of that

> place and culture. I'm not part of the traditions so I feel alienated even though I'm surrounded by it. It's actually easier not being in it. I want to be in it but I can't. There are so many differences between them even places they go on holidays and things they do and where they shop ... The Catholic flags up here would offend me but the Union Jack wouldn't because I was brought up in that way. I don't know why I feel like that. I had no choice growing up so I don't see me as who I want to be. I'd like to be a part of the Protestant culture openly but I have too much background now. I took the easy way because of what I knew but that's not what I want now but I can't openly be that because of the past.
> *(Mother of child in need)*

Feeling different in the community

Almost half of all the parents interviewed felt that cross-community families were identified by others in the community as being different. For this reason many families chose to move away from their own community to a neutral area where no one knew about their cross-community background. Relocating to other areas was not possible for all families, especially those living in public housing. It is possible that NIMMA families have more choice in this respect.

> We decided to move here ... this was a neutral area. I think we couldn't have lived near either of our families because it would have been frowned upon and it would have been too much for us.
> *(Mother, NIMMA)*

> It was very much a sense of 'We will distance geographically.' I think we did make that deliberate decision. There was an extra reason for staying away from home now. We knew our parents would probably not want anybody to know.
> *(Father, NIMMA)*

Many families remained in segregated housing areas and were often wary of disclosing their cross-community background. Disguising their cross-community background was easier if their children were raised in one religious belief.

> I moved when I met him. I don't think they even knew what religion I was. You know if somebody spoke to me in the street I'd speak back, we never brought religion into it. The children were all raised Catholic so they assumed I was too.
> **(Mother of looked after child)**

Parents who felt different in their community were usually concerned about their family's safety.

> I got a brick thrown at me by a twelve-year-old cos the kids have a Catholic name and they were being called Fenian Bastards. The children know all about their background and they know not to talk about it. Children get slagged and slapped.
> **(Mother of child in need)**

This was particularly pertinent when one parent had previously been involved in Loyalist or Republican activities as explained by this father, who had a background within Loyalism and now lived in a Catholic area.

> Even yet I get a lot of stick and certain people would be wary. We lived in a Republican area first of all and never had bother. They just watched us at the start … There was no paramilitary problems there but if you needed water on a Loyalist estate nobody would give it to you … I feel safe enough and I'm finished with all that [Loyalism] now. At times when there's trouble you'd be thinking about it because you never know so you'd be on your guard then.
> **(Father of child in need)**

Overall, almost three-quarters of all parents interviewed felt that cross-community families are at greater risk of intimidation or violence. Indeed, almost half of all parents had experienced intimidation or violence because they were a cross-community family. This included four parents of looked after children, four parents of children in need and two parents from NIMMA. As the following quotations illustrate, families from all social classes experienced intimidation and violence:

> We were threatened out of our first house. They told me I had to get out because I had turned. They called me scum. I suppose I was a stranger. I wasn't from there. Then we

moved to [Catholic area]. We were there for over a year before we told people and then there were no problems cos they seen me going to Mass and the children at the ceremonies ... I had that with my husband at home as well though. He would call me an Orange bastard and the older one's heard that. From time to time [oldest child] would say that and him and [younger child] have fought about that. He called me that at a christening and the police had to be called because they fought ... Protestants and Catholics together face a lot more because they have it from both sides. There's always enough of a minority to keep it going.
(Mother of looked after child)

I think there are class issues with that in relation to where you can live ... I think it's still there but people in more middle or upper classes are very polite about it. With segregation everyone experiences sectarianism.
(Father, NIMMA)

Actually my husband had come up to visit me and our neighbour nearly murdered him one night for being this Fenian.
(Mother of looked after child)

We were put out of our last home. It was a mainly Protestant area. We had broken windows and the children were having nightmares.
(Mother of child in need)

Deciding about child's religion

Almost one third of parents interviewed indicated that deciding about their children's religious upbringing was particularly difficult. Figure 3.1 illustrates how parents in this study had made the decision. In ten cases the child's mother made this decision and in four cases the child's father did. However, six parents felt they made the decision together and a further four suggested they made the decision together taking the views of their families into consideration. One couple felt they had decided on their child's religion because of pressure from clergy. Another couple reared their children with no religious identity allowing them to decide for themselves when they were older. They felt their children were aware of religious divisions in Northern Ireland and would identify themselves as 'nothing' rather than being cross-community.

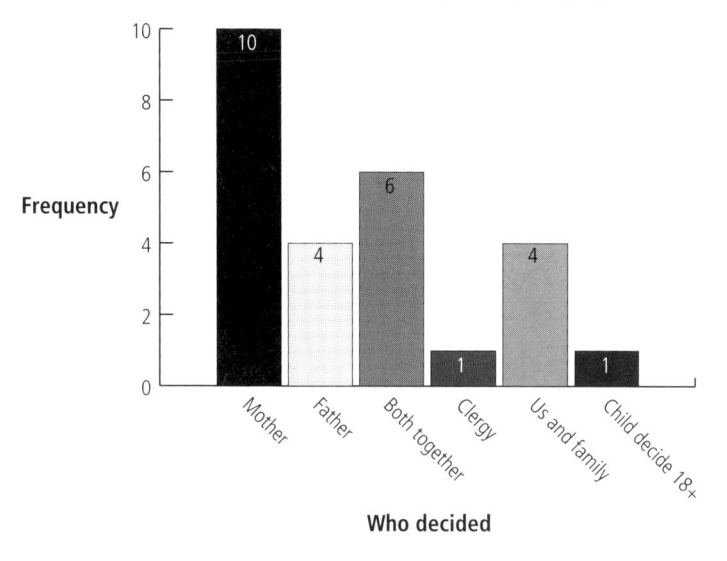

Figure 3.1 Who makes decisions about children's religious upbringing

Who decided	Frequency
Mother	10
Father	4
Both together	6
Clergy	1
Us and family	4
Child decide 18+	1

Parents found making decisions about their child's religious upbringing difficult for various reasons: they had to find a middle ground between their individual beliefs; pressure from clergy and family; or one parent had to accept the other parent's decision.

> My husband insisted they would all be brought up Catholic. There was no choice for me. I was only seventeen or eighteen but it was very selfish of him looking back. He should have thought about the issues first. It was just later near the end of the pregnancy he said the children will be Catholic and that's it.
> *(Mother of looked after child)*

> There was rows about it and then their dad just insisted. My mum said that if daddy was alive they would have been Protestant because he wouldn't have allowed them to be Catholic. My folks weren't happy about it.
> *(Mother of looked after child)*

> The priest said we have to be Roman Catholic and we agreed
> but you can still go your own way. We weren't really happy
> about it but we didn't care because we did our own thing.
> *(Father of looked after child)*

Almost all of the parents who felt it was not difficult explained this was because one parent had accepted the other parent's decision without disagreement.

> It was just me. I insisted they were Catholic baptism. There
> was no uproar.
> *(Mother of looked after child)*

> When I was pregnant with the first I told my husband that
> they would be baptised Catholic. I haven't been to church in
> years but I just think it's nice for children to be baptised
> from original sin and everything.
> *(Mother of child in need)*

> He didn't mind so I got him baptised. I'd be staunch
> Catholic. The Catholic religion is very important to me.
> *(Mother of looked after child)*

Four parents felt it was not difficult to decide about their children's religious upbringing because they had a mutual understanding that both of their religious backgrounds had to be respected. Interestingly, these four parents were from NIMMA and overall only one parent from NIMMA found it hard to make these decisions. As mentioned previously, children from NIMMA were more likely to identify with being Interchurch or be baptised alternately, therefore, these parents did not have to decide against one parent's religious background.

> We generally started off with God and Christianity. We are in
> the position of being able to explain to them what we
> individually believe but sometimes saying that there is a fair
> range of belief … It is getting that sense of essential values
> and integrity.
> *(Mother, NIMMA)*

> We did both. We celebrated baptism etcetera simultaneously.
> In fact the clergy have got into trouble with their bishops
> because we had mixed ceremonies. Our children would have
> been Christian. People often confuse Protestant and

Catholic as different religions but they are both denominations of the Christian faith ... We openly talked about religion and prayers and we took them to services. We were also involved in NIMMA and Corrymeela so they thought everyone did.
(Father, NIMMA)

They were baptised alternately ... they're ambidextrous, you know, they're not the sort of people that will be single-minded. I mean we would probably go to both churches and they might go to one or the other. We weren't fixated on it but then they would have been confirmed and taken communion in their own respective churches. So they have a definite identity. We talked about it at home and were very open about it. They would have been at home in both churches.
(Mother, NIMMA)

Figure 3.2 shows that the majority of parents made decisions about their children's religious upbringing after the birth of their child. Only one couple discussed this early in their relationship, four at their engagement, one at their marriage and one shortly after marriage. These findings suggest that many parents are faced with deciding about their children's religious identity following their birth without previously discussing this with their partner.

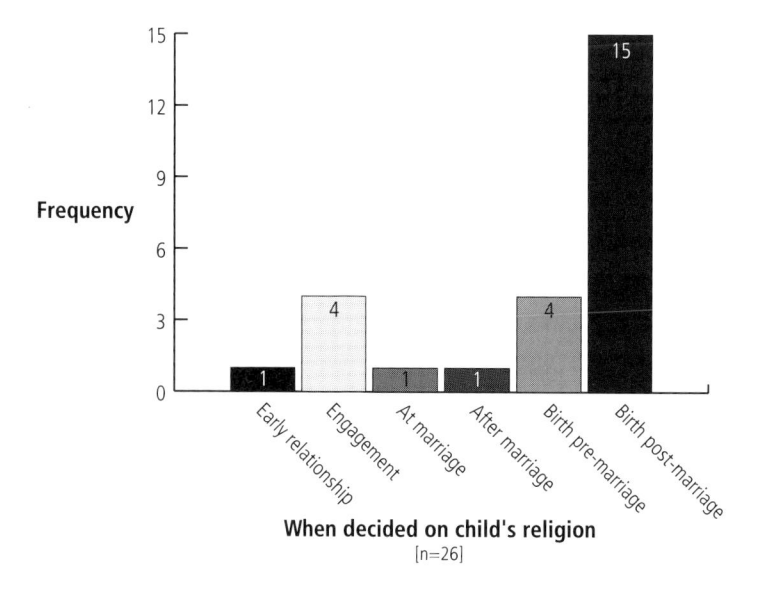

Figure 3.2 When parents decide about children's religious upbringing

When decided on child's religion	Frequency
Early relationship	1
Engagement	4
At marriage	1
After marriage	1
Birth pre-marriage	4
Birth post-marriage	15

[n=26]

Most parents felt that cross-community children were under pressure to choose one religious identity because of the likelihood of discrimination and pressures related to living in a segregated society:

> Oh definitely, from family, but we didn't give in. We needed to compromise between us and be independent. I think it is because you are maybe more aware of what priests in particular might say to you.
> *(Father, NIMMA)*

> Regularly from the clergy and from our families. The baptism was a big pressure. There was a big argument and we got no replies. In the end when he was three years old it was a Roman Catholic baptism with the Church of Ireland clergy there.
> *(Father, NIMMA)*

One of the couples from NIMMA decided to raise their children as Catholic because of this pressure although they would have preferred their children to be raised as Interchurch. Another couple felt maintaining a dual religious identity would, in practice, have been too burdensome:

> That was a bit of a worry as to whether you could do it [be Interchurch] or not, if you could do it successfully or not. I think probably the thought of having to go to two services every Sunday was just a bit heavy duty.
> *(Mother, NIMMA)*

This parent decided to baptise her children alternately and she was concerned that she should have made more efforts for her children to have a deeper understanding of both religious backgrounds:

> I suppose they have thought of it as normal because that's what kids do until the world outside tells them it's not normal. I was kind of surprised. I thought because I could tell the difference that they could tell the difference, but they couldn't. The churches are quite divided, and being in a mixed marriage you become very sensitive to any insensitivities especially your own church, you kind of excuse it from strangers but I would have found the role in promoting their identity a bit of a challenge.
> *(Mother, NIMMA)*

However, some parents of children who were raised in both religious faiths felt their children could be confused about their identity because communities in Northern Ireland are so segregated:

> They don't fit into a category although that's constantly around them. I think it's confusing for them. So on the negative side they are targeted because of their name and confused by it. They live it every day even though they wouldn't think automatically Catholic or Protestant. On the positive they have no bitterness of one or the other and aren't growing up feeling superior over another. They don't label people on their religion.
> ***(Mother of child in need)***

Parents were also particularly worried when their children had developed very strong political beliefs or sectarian attitudes:

> We would have rows and discussions about it. He is having very political views now that he gets from his friends and some of his dad's family. He wouldn't get that in my house.
> I think he's strong willed and he likes to be different from the rest of the family. He likes to be appreciated as a big man because he's a teenager now. I would worry more about him. The other children would be known by both sides of the community but he would only be known by the Catholic side so Protestant contacts would see him as bad, as a Fenian and he's a teenager at a Catholic school from a Catholic area.
> ***(Mother of child in need)***

Making decisions about school

Figure 3.3 shows that the majority of children involved in this study attended segregated schools.

Figure 3.3 Type of school children attend

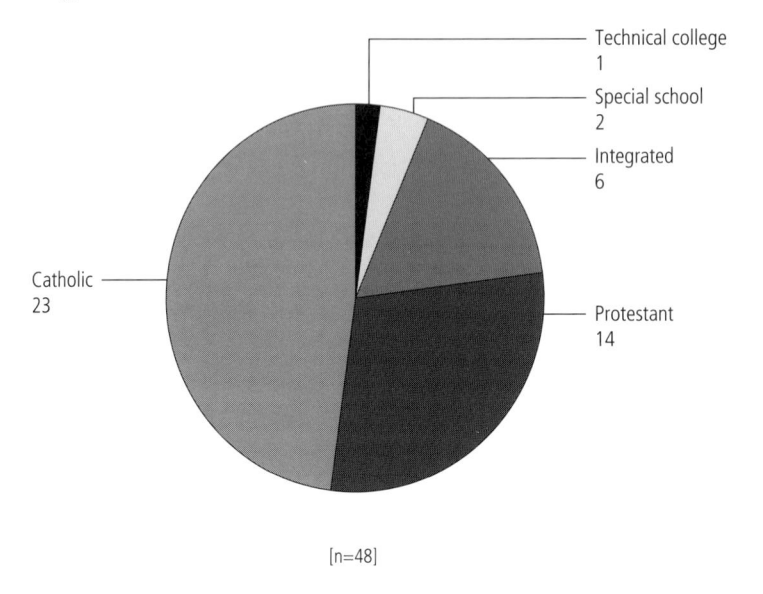

- Technical college 1
- Special school 2
- Integrated 6
- Protestant 14
- Catholic 23

[n=48]

Parents usually chose the most local school or the school that matched their children's religious upbringing if they were raised in one religious faith. Many parents generally felt they had no option since they did not have access to local integrated schools.

> Well they were Catholic then so they just went to the Catholic school.
> *(Mother of looked after child)*

> There were no places in [integrated school]. There's not enough integrated schools.
> *(Mother of looked after child)*

> They went to Protestant schools. Although we got married in the chapel [Catholic church] the Protestant school was beside us and the priest had been so unhelpful.
> *(Mother of looked after child)*

Some parents had initially disagreed about which school their child should attend:

> When he was going to school he insisted he should go to a Protestant school but I said I had him and I want him at a Catholic school. He accepted that eventually.
> **(Mother of looked after child)**

Parents from NIMMA described some of their children's experiences at school. These included being rejected by their peers and attending extra classes outside school for religious teaching. All of the parents from NIMMA strongly supported integrated education for all children, however two parents recommended that staff at integrated schools should give more consideration to children who come from cross-community families rather than assuming everyone has one religious identity.

> We went to see both masters in the Catholic school and the state school. The master at the Catholic school wouldn't speak to us because they felt a Catholic school was for Catholic children… So they went to the other school and we organised classes for youngsters at home with Catholic teachers so they got their Catholic education as well. Then they went to the integrated college.
> **(Mother, NIMMA)**

> In the particular [integrated] school they go to there are two separate religions up until fourth year. [daughter] had chose to go into the Protestant RE because it was better for her at school then it was perceived that she was a Protestant but then come to the first holy day she decided she wanted to go to Mass and someone asked why was she there… now the children are put down as RC or Methodist so that has actually pleased us because at least it is recognised that that's what we had originally put down. We used to be classed as 'Other'!
> **(Father, NIMMA)**

Parental perspectives in children's experience of being cross-community

According to their parents, all of the NIMMA children had mixed friendships, however only one third of the children in need sample had. Parents who felt their children only had friends from one religious background explained this was because they attended segregated schools or lived in segregated areas that restricted cross-community contact. Parents also noted that there were limited opportunities for their children to participate in integrated social activities. Others explained that their children were afraid to meet people from the other religious backgrounds:

> He won't visit Protestant friends in their area because he doesn't feel safe but they can come here. He refuses to buy Reebok trainers as well because they have a union jack design on the back. His friends wear ones like that but he won't because he would get a slagging.
> *(Mother of child in need)*

> I think they're mainly Catholic there at school or Protestant at his granny's. He won't go out here himself unless I'm with him more or less because of all the trouble and there's young ones when the milkman comes round they ask for eight or nine milk bottles you know to throw. He's a bit afraid, when they see the police van they start off [throwing the bottles] you know and it scares him.
> *(Mother of child in need)*

More than half of all parents felt their children had negative experiences because they were from a cross-community background. These experiences were usually related to being bullied or teased by peers:

> My children have had quite a few experiences now. [son] got beat up himself at the bottom of the street but he invited trouble up to a point but he was called a Fenian. [daughter] got tortured and one day she was pinned up against that wall and they were giving her abuse about being a Fenian. She was tormented … I mean she was absolutely tortured.
> *(Mother of looked after child)*

> It would have been the attitude. It was just such ignorance and bigotry right through because everything's segregated. When [daughter] went to the Catholic school she had taken up with this Catholic girl and then [second daughter] was born just after and her friend came in and said, 'oh well Catholics breed like rabbits', at the age of eleven. This girl stopped being her friend. But in [son's] primary school, a nice boy went home and said to his mother 'What's a Catholic?' and one day he went into the classroom and announced 'Well he's in the IRA.' It's not heavy stuff but it's stupid and he found it quite difficult … there was a total lack of understanding and I can understand it, but the children have said it's alright because we talked about it at home so they were given a language to explain it and this is where I think a mixed marriage, you must engage with it, you can't say it doesn't matter, you've got to give them the wherewithal to cope with the questions and you've got to be prepared to listen to what they are getting thrown at them.
> **(Mother, NIMMA)**

Parents who felt their children did not have any negative experiences suggested this was because their children identified with one religious background and were viewed by others as being either Catholic or Protestant rather than cross-community. The majority of parents felt their child had both positive and negative experiences because they were from a cross-community background. Positives included being more informed about religious diversity, open-minded, non-sectarian and less prejudiced:

> I remember when they went to school my son came home and told me he had been asked was he Protestant or Catholic and he didn't know because really the answer was yes. He thought it was sad that there was only one church for other children. So we think it was positive for both of them.
> **(Father, NIMMA)**

> They don't see themselves as Catholic. They don't fit into a category although that's constantly around them … I think it's confusing for them. So on the negative side they are targeted because of their name and confused by it. They live

> it every day even though they wouldn't think automatically Catholic or Protestant. On the positive they have no bitterness of one or the other and aren't growing up feeling superior over another. They don't label people on their religion.
> *(Mother of child in need)*

Summary

Cross-community families living in Northern Ireland face a range of discriminatory barriers. First, negative family reactions to their relationship have the potential to reduce informal family support networks. Second, actually getting married and finding somewhere safe to live was very difficult. Third, cross-community families often experienced pressure for one parent to change their religious identity or keep their religious identity a secret. Fourth, cross-community families were more likely to experience intimidation and violence. Finally, parents also had to make crucial decisions about children's religious upbringing and attendance at segregated schools that were often very difficult. Parents acknowledged that their children had mixed experiences of being cross-community and were restricted by the pervasiveness of segregated educational, environmental and social systems. All of these stressors on cross-community families had a direct impact on cross-community families. Findings indicate that for parents of looked after children these stressors had a detrimental effect on their ability to keep their family safe and maintain strong family relationships, highlighting the importance of providing effective support services for these families.

4. Children's experiences of being cross-community

This chapter discusses children's perceptions of their religious identity and their experiences of being from a cross-community family. It explores what children see as the positive and negative aspects of their cross-community status, especially the impact of living in a segregated society on opportunities they have to maintain a dual identity and establish mixed friendships.

Children's views on their religious identity

Figure 4.1 depicts children's perceptions of their religious identity. The majority of children identified with the Catholic faith and a small minority, all from NIMMA, described themselves as Interchurch. Interestingly, only looked after children were unsure about their religious identity or viewed themselves as atheists. Indeed, seven out of the 34 looked after children involved in this study were unaware that their parents had different religious backgrounds.

Figure 4.1 Children's religious identity

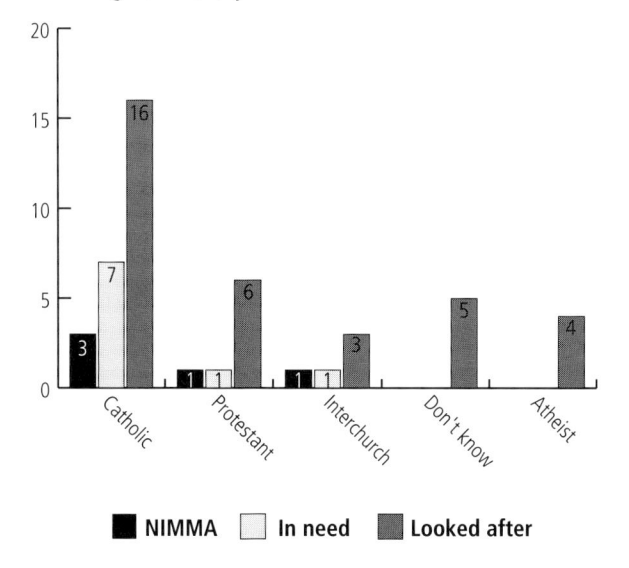

	Catholic	Protestant	Interchurch	Don't know	Atheist
NIMMA	3	1	1		
In need	7	1	1		
Looked after	16	6	3	5	4

The children as a group had mixed views about the importance of religion, with almost the same number reporting that religion was very important or important (26) as those who saw it as not important or not at all important (25). However, there were considerable differences between the views of the different groups of children, as shown in Figure 4.2.

Interestingly, adding the ten looked after children who felt religion was not important at all and six children who deemed it to be not important, almost half of looked after children felt religion was of no importance. Similarly, almost all of the children in need felt religion was either not important or not important at all. However, only one child from NIMMA felt religion was not important at all, with the remaining ten children from NIMMA deeming religion as important or very important. This illustrates the difference in attitudes towards religion between children from NIMMA and children in need or looked after.

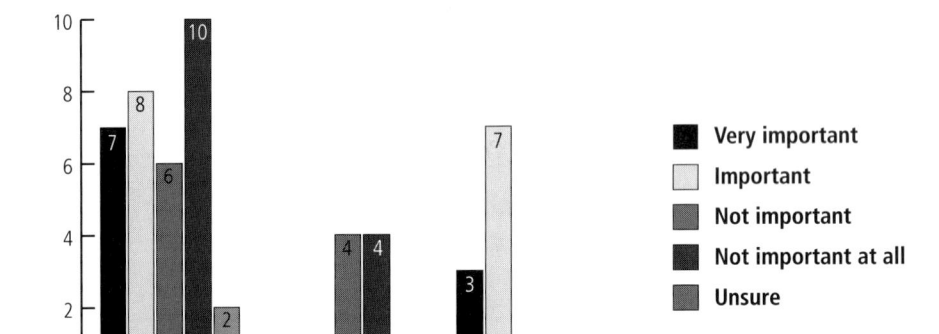

Figure 4.2 Children's views on the importance of religion

As the following quotations illustrate, children who felt religion was important explained that this was because it was part of their identity or their family background and it was what they believed in:

> It's important to your beliefs. You'd be all confused if you didn't know what you believe in.
> *(14-year-old female – foster care)*
>
> Because it's about Jesus and Jesus helps us to live properly.
> *(7-year-old female – NIMMA)*

> I like going to Mass. I like talking about it and in the morning at school.
> ***(Ten-year-old male – child in need)***

> Because it becomes a part of your life. It's your and your parents' beliefs. It's what you are in a way.
> ***(16-year-old female – NIMMA)***

Children who felt religion was not important explained this that was because people were equal regardless of their religious identity and religion caused so much strife in Northern Ireland. Here, children seem to be thinking of religion as part of community identity as much as a belief system.

> Because it's one less person that's not bitter. People like me are a lot better because you shouldn't need to worry about it. We all worship the same God.
> ***(19-year-old female – foster care)***

> It's really stupid and causes a lot of fights. It would be better if there was no religion or only one religion or just forget about it and get on with life.
> ***(14-year-old female – home on Care Order)***

> Everyone's the same so I don't think it makes any difference.
> ***(17-year-old male – residential care)***

> They're both rotten. I don't like it. It's stupid.
> ***(Nine-year-old male – child in need)***

> It's about who people are, not what they are.
> ***(15-year-old female – child in need)***

Several children felt that being discriminated against by both sides at different times of their lives had 'put them off' religion:

> I was reared Catholic but I wouldn't class myself or [son] as anything. He can when he's older. I've been living in different places and you get hassle from people that put me off religion … You got kickings because your mum was Catholic and my home got attacked because they never knew my dad.
> ***(21-year-old female – leaving care)***

Some children explained that although they identified with one religion they also supported the other side:

> I used to go to church. I believe in the Bible teaching and it's different from Catholics. I go to the Twelfth band parades but I really support both sides because I go to the St Paddy day things too.
> *(19-year-old female – foster care)*

> If you were choosing your religion what would you choose?
> Both. I'd sorta like to be my mum and my dad.
> *(nine-year-old male – NIMMA)*

However, being cross-community in a segregated society meant that children often had to change their religious identity depending on who they were with and what area they were in:

> I'm just half and half. I say I'm Protestant if I'm hanging around with Protestants. If I'm down Dad's way I say I'm Catholic cos it's a Catholic area. I don't really care.
> *(14-year-old male – residential care)*

> *Interviewer: Would you tell your friends your parents are both?*
> I would only tell close friends.
> *(11-year-old female – child in need)*

> It's weird [being cross-community]. I don't know what to say when people ask me so I say both but then they don't believe me. I'm a Catholic to Mum and a Protestant to Dad. Daddy was an orangeman so I'm half orange and half green, white and gold.
> *(Nine-year-old male – child in need)*

Only children from NIMMA identified themselves as Interchurch and these children outlined the benefits of following both Protestant and Catholic faiths.

> I went to both church and Mass. I'm still both so I would call myself a Christian … There a bits I like in both. Some weeks I don't go and other weeks I go to each at different times. In the Church of Ireland I would help and serve at the altar or else I go to Mass because it's only up the road. I'm glad to

> be in both because I have more of a clue about both and don't think of Protestant or Catholic as the other religion.
> *(19-year-old female – NIMMA)*

> I'm both Methodist and Catholic – Interchurch is the word used to explain it. Most weeks I go to a service either the Methodist one or the Catholic one.
> *(14-year-old female – NIMMA)*

Children's experiences of being cross-community

Children's descriptions of their experience of being cross-community reflect the parental perspectives described earlier. Children from the NIMMA focus group suggested that the most important things for young people from cross-community backgrounds were:

- personal safety in segregated areas and times of the year when sectarian divisions were heightened
- avoiding sectarian activity such as riots
- having support from family and friends
- being allowed to choose their religious identity
- having opportunity to maintain a dual identity
- experiencing both sides of their religious and cultural backgrounds
- accessing integrated services, including integrated schools.

Generally, children from this focus group felt that living in a mainly segregated society made being cross-community more difficult:

> You feel different if it's one sided but if you're in an integrated place like an integrated school it's easier.
> *(NIMMA, focus group)*

Figure 4.3 shows that out of the 48 children interviewed, 19 children felt there were both good and less good things about being cross-community, five children only identified good things and, in contrast, seven children felt there were only less good things.

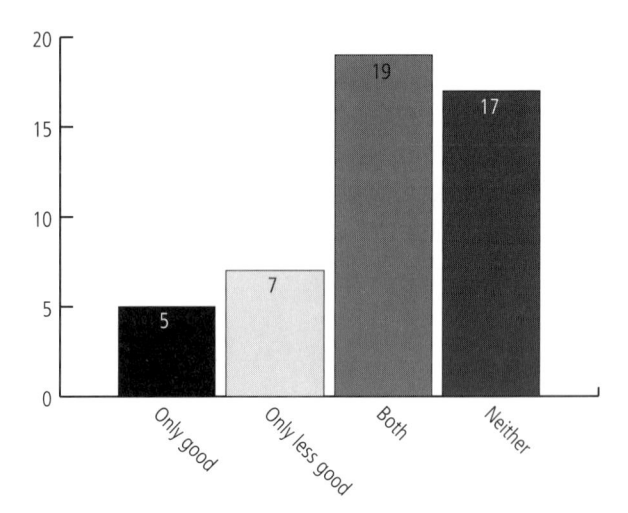

Figure 4.3 Children's views on positive or negative aspects of being cross-community

Category	Count
Only good	5
Only less good	7
Both	19
Neither	17

Of the 48 children, 17 did not feel there was anything good or less good about being cross-community. Of these children seven were not sure if they were from a cross-community background and the remaining ten suggested that being cross-community made no difference at all:

> There is no good nor bad in it, it's just my mum and dad,
> I don't care what they are.
> *(13-year-old male – residential care)*

The main positive aspects that children identified with being cross-community were being informed about both religious and cultural backgrounds, being less biased and being able to develop friendships with people from both sides of the community:

> You're able to learn about both faiths and don't have a prejudiced view of either faith. And being able to choose if you want to remain Interchurch or become one faith.
> *(16-year-old female – NIMMA)*

> You meet different people who come from different backgrounds and make new friends by going to NIMMA weekends. It helps you understand more than one religion.
> *(14-year-old female – NIMMA)*

One looked after child explained that being exposed to both religious and cultural backgrounds was positive but could also create tensions in relationships with one parent:

> Mum keeps buying Catholic stuff for me and Dad does Protestant stuff … Mum bought me green, white and gold coloured phone cover as well and my Dad got me a red, white and blue one with the UVF red hand.
> *Interviewer: Which one do you use?*
> I use the green, white and gold one
> *Interviewer: And what do you tell your dad?*
> I'm a Catholic and I'm not going to walk around in here with the one he got me. I only use one, and he said sorry.
> *(13-year-old male – residential care)*

The less good aspects were experiencing sectarian discrimination within their family and the community, not being able to discuss both religious backgrounds with their family and friends, family disagreements about religion and culture, feeling confused about their identity, dealing with assumptions people made about their identity and lacking access to cross-community cultural activities. The quotations below demonstrate how these impacted on children's lives:

> Not being allowed to talk about your religion to the other parent. If I go to Mum's area it's a Protestant area and I would get hidings if they know I'm a Catholic.
> *(16-year-old female – residential care)*

> Listening to people expressing bitter comments about both the Protestant and Catholic religions, and being unable to defend either because of a risk of a beating.
> *(19-year-old female – foster care)*

> There would be more rows in our family. Brothers and sisters may fight or fall out. Maybe one calling the other Protestant. And rows between the mother and father about wanting to go to Mass and the other wouldn't want to.
> *(16-year-old male – foster care)*

> Problems with family members who cannot accept you and worries about what strangers might think.
> *(16-year-old female – NIMMA)*

> My dad wanted us to do Irish dancing and we weren't allowed to watch English TV. He wanted us to be 100 per cent Irish. He was sectarian. If he didn't die you wouldn't find things the same – we'd all be speaking Irish. My brother's sectarian too and he goes to marches and all. He was in children's homes a lot for about eleven or twelve years but he's not anymore and he's not seriously like that now he just wanted to be like his Da. I don't think Da would've married Mum if she didn't turn Catholic.
> *(14-year-old female – home on Care Order)*

> Well there's a lot of bitterness between the two of them. I know my mum hates my dad because he's Catholic and she'll say we shouldn't go with Catholic boys or have Catholic friends or go near our Catholic family – shouldn't mix. Just I'm from a very sectarian family. I don't know why she went with my Dad – why she done that if she was so against Catholics – it didn't last long anyway.
> *(19-year-old female – foster care)*

Of 34 looked after children interviewed, 13 felt they had a negative experience at school related to being from a cross-community family. This was usually being teased or bullied by peers at school. Children who attended segregated schools found that other people assumed they were from one religious background because of the school they attended:

> It's an all Protestant school so they think you're Protestant and if you live in a Protestant area they think you're Protestant. They would see all the flags and what everybody's saying and fighting with Catholics.
> *(15-year-old female – foster care)*

> I went to an Irish Language primary school. A lot of kids' parents were in jail and were Republicans so I would have preferred not to have went there. At primary school it was a big deal. No one knew about me though. At primary school they would have assumed I was Catholic. I wasn't offended

> by the assumption but I was annoyed by the narrow teaching they had and not learning about other things.
> *(19-year-old female – NIMMA)*

Being affiliated with one religious background became a particular problem when these children came into contact with peers who were from the other community background:

> Because of my name they would assume we're Catholic but I have always told them about Mum and Dad. One boy gave out [verbal abuse] one time and I fought with him. My sister and me could always defend each other.
> *(19-year-old female – foster care)*

> The boys at the other school start fights outside the school just because we're Catholic and they're Protestant. I stay away from it … They'd see by the uniform and everything or if you were wearing a Celtic top I think you feel aware.
> *(17-year-old male – residential care)*

Children preferred to attend integrated schools and the minority that did felt that the best thing about their school was the fact that it was integrated:

> The best thing is that it is mixed boys and girls of all religions and pupils come from different areas … you don't get involved in fights about religion or you don't do anything stupid.
> *(17-year-old male – foster care)*

However, children who attended integrated schools were doubly disadvantaged outside school as people from both sides of the community assumed they were from the other side:

> They don't know but they still get battered because they assume and they think that more Catholics go to the integrated school than Protestants. I would say that our school has more Catholic pupils in it than Protestant. I am not too sure but I think so.
> *(17-year-old male – foster care)*

> They think you might be Protestant and Catholic. They thought I went to church every day and thought I was religious so they didn't play with me.
> *(11-year-old male – home on Care Order)*

The salient effects of religion on peer relationships

Religious or community identity may also impact on children's friendships. Investigation of this produced other information on friendships more generally. Rather distressingly, one looked after child felt they did not have any friends. Worryingly, this child was living in a residential home for disabled adults. Almost one third of looked after children felt they did not have a best friend and only three children living in residential care felt they had friends where they were living. One child living in residential care stated:

> I never had mates in here because I hate them.
> *(14-year-old male – residential care)*

As shown in Figure 4.4, only five out of 34 looked after children had friends from both Catholic and Protestant religious backgrounds. Eight children did not know the religious background of their friends and some of these children indicated it was not appropriate to ask their friends about that:

> I shouldn't know their religion. It doesn't matter what church they go to. If you go to church or chapel it doesn't matter as long as you go.
> *(11-year-old male – foster care)*

> I wouldn't want to know … it might not be any of my business.
> *(Ten-year-old female – foster care)*

Figure 4.4 Religious background of looked after children's friends

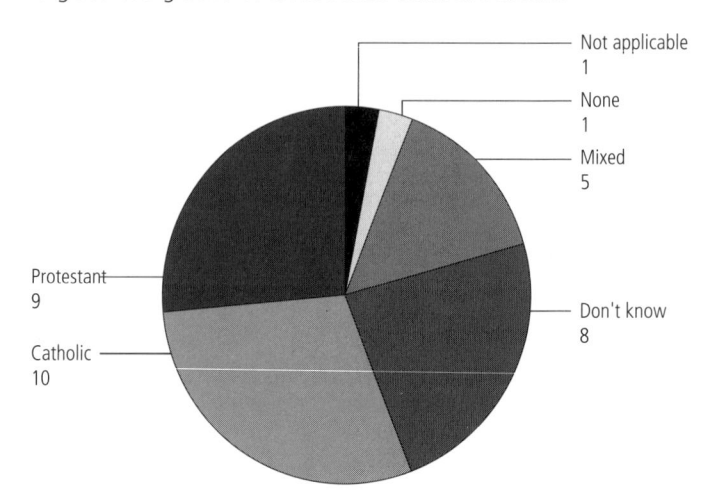

- Not applicable: 1
- None: 1
- Mixed: 5
- Don't know: 8
- Catholic: 10
- Protestant: 9

Of 15 foster carers, nine suggested the children in their care had mixed friendships. They felt this was possible because they lived in mixed areas or had taught children in their care to be open to cross-community friendships. Those who felt children in their care did not have mixed friendships explained that this was mainly due to segregated educational systems and housing areas.

Residential social workers emphasised that the most important peer contact for children living in residential care was with other young people in that home. They felt this subculture within residential homes was the strongest influence on peer relationships and suggested that peer contact was easier for cross-community children who had chosen one religious identity or none:

> He was brought up in a Catholic area in the Catholic religion … It would be the first time in his life he's mixed with Protestants in residential care.
> *(Field Social Worker)*

> They wouldn't have a huge peer group outside the home. They lose contact with friends and I don't know if that makes a difference. There is a subculture here because they have spent their life surviving and have to put aside their beliefs to suit the peer group in the home and friends from beforehand are no longer prioritised which can be unhealthy. It's more about surviving in the peer group of the residential home and minimally about learning and social skills so they could feel like misfits.
> *(Residential Social Worker)*

Indeed, five social workers explained that cross-community children often hid information about one part of their identity from their peers:

> His mother lives in a Protestant area but his own friends would be Catholic from where he lives now. So he would only have social contacts on one side of the fence. I advise them to try and avoid situations like that if possible and protect themselves and give them answers that are non-committal but you know that's an added pressure on children. Maybe at school too because you don't have to be a genius to find out about these sorts of things and it could be a problem if it's the wrong religion.

> *Interviewer: Do you feel some of them try to hide part of their identity?*
> Oh definitely.
> *(Field Social Worker)*

> Actually the children themselves, or the young people themselves, protect themselves. It is measured by the school. So they don't say 'Look my Dad is Protestant, I'm a Catholic.' Their response would be 'I'm a Catholic and I go to a Catholic school' and that is how they would perceive it.
> *(Residential Social Worker)*

Concurring with the views of their parents and carers, children who only have friends from one religious background explained this was because schools, social spaces and housing areas are segregated:

> They're Protestant because of the school we went to. A few boys give [a Catholic friend] abuse when I'm with him and call me Fenian. I've got a few kickings because of that and got into rows because I go to a Protestant youth club.
> *(17-year-old male – foster care)*

> They're mostly Catholics because there's only five Protestants round here.
> *(14-year-old female – foster care)*

Overall, the majority of children suggested that the religious background of their friends was not important. Typical comments children made were:

> Everybody's the same. If he was black I'd like him the same. You go for someone who's dead on and who'd help you if you were in need, not religion.
> *(17-year-old male – foster care)*

> We don't care about religion, we don't worry about it either, we do our work and get on with our lives, and I don't care.
> *(Ten-year-old male – foster care)*

> It shouldn't be an issue. It should be your personality and things you have in common.
> *(16-year-old female – NIMMA)*

However, although these children felt religious background was not important, they were acutely aware of the need to negotiate identities carefully in the presence of people from different religious backgrounds and in different community areas.

> It doesn't bother me but it would be difficult to talk about the troubles. Sometimes you forget they're there and start slabbering and then we fall out sometimes about it. When we meet in the town it's no bother because it's mixed.
> *(15-year-old female – foster care)*

> Not important at all … I know the difference between Catholics and Protestants and I understand it. I know what not to say if I don't know about other religions.
> *(17-year-old male – foster care)*

> I like being with Catholics but I'd also like being with Protestants, but I go to a Catholic church which is very Catholic, they don't like Protestants … but I do because that's my dad, he was one.
> *(11-year-old female – residential care)*

> It's not really important. I don't care and I just play with my friends. A lot of my friends judge people like who are this and that. Just all the bad stuff about them … I don't listen to them I just walk away.
> *(11-year-old male – foster care)*

Only seven children felt their friend's religious background was important. These children explained that this was because: they had to respect their friend's religious beliefs; it was important they had the same religion so they had things in common; or it was safer to only maintain friendships with people from the same religious background.

> He likes the same as me so he's Catholic. He'd be bored if I'm not and then I'd have no one to play with. Religion is usually important to us and we talk about it outside.
> *(Ten-year-old male – child in need)*

> I'd rather hang around with Catholics – they're not as bad … most Protestants fire stones and carry on like that.
> *(16-year-old male – foster care)*

Twelve young people had a boyfriend or girlfriend. The majority of these young people felt that personality and compatibility were more important than religious background:

> If I like her and she was Catholic it wouldn't stop me.
> *(17-year-old male – foster care)*

> I was seeing a Catholic before … It doesn't bother me. We laughed about it.
> *(14-year-old male – residential care)*

> Because it doesn't matter – there's no difference between us. Catholic and Protestant is just a name.
> *(17-year-old female – foster care)*

> It doesn't matter and your parents can't say anything because they were mixed.
> *(NIMMA, focus group)*

However, two young people felt the religious background of their partner was important because of sectarianism, peer pressure, family expectations or the importance of having common interests. Indeed, other young people who deemed it to be unimportant also concurred that being in a cross-community relationship would be more difficult.

> I've been out with a few Catholics and it doesn't really bother me – there just seemed to be a lot of complications in it. But my mum used to have told us to stick to our own because she had big problems round that … It's a wee bit more important in schools because when you get older and turning the other side you'd have all of the problems of what's going on.
> *(19-year-old female – foster care)*

> It wouldn't be important to me but it would be to the girl's mum. It is not that they are worried about it but say I went to live in [Protestant area] it would be a risk for me. And it would be important to my friends. They wouldn't like it if she was Protestant.
> *(17-year-old male – foster care)*

Cross-community children's views on integration

Overall, almost half of the children interviewed were members of social or leisure clubs. These clubs included Young Women's Club, Air Cadets, Christian clubs, Boys' and Girls' Brigade, youth clubs, sports clubs, after-school clubs and Extern (a voluntary organisation in Northern Ireland). The majority of children felt that religious identity was unimportant to them at these clubs. Only two children felt religion is important at clubs. In one case, this was because he attended Boys' Brigade where he felt everyone must be Protestant and in the other, everyone at the child's local youth club wore Rangers shirts. However, Figure 4.5 shows that children had mixed views about how important religious background is to others at clubs they attended, but in general they thought religion was more important to others than to them.

> They don't get along with Catholics. They completely hate Catholics.
> *(15-year-old female – foster care)*

> After school clubs for football … no people from the [Republic area] can come, it has to be people in school that go, so Catholics couldn't come because they're not at my school.
> *(12-year-old male – residential care)*

Figure 4.5 Importance of religion to other people at social and leisure clubs

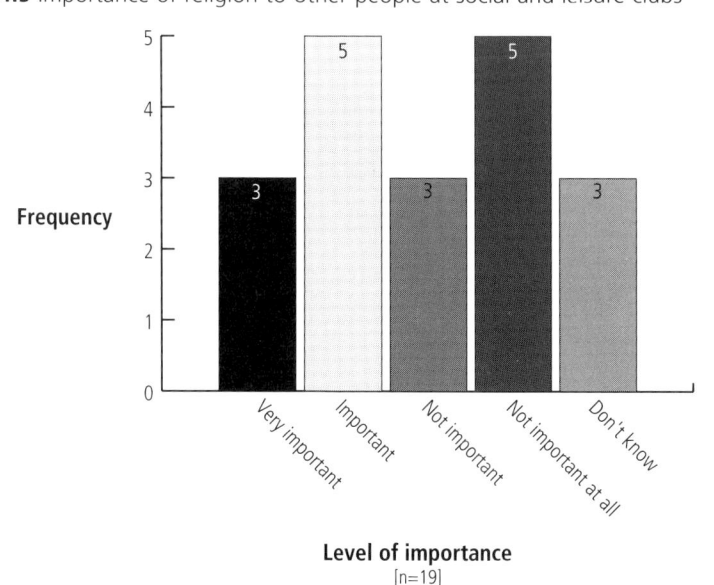

Level of importance	Frequency
Very important	3
Important	5
Not important	3
Not important at all	5
Don't know	3

[n=19]

Children were asked if they felt social clubs, schools and housing areas should integrate Catholics and Protestants or stay segregated. Figure 4.6 shows that the majority of children preferred integration in all three settings.

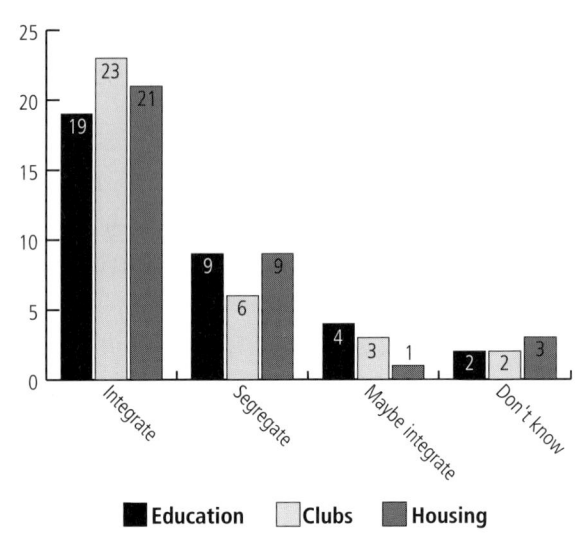

Figure 4.6 Children's views on integration

	Integrate	Segregate	Maybe integrate	Don't know
Education	19	9	4	2
Clubs	23	6	3	2
Housing	21	9	1	3

The majority of children suggested that schools and social clubs should be integrated because people should have an opportunity to meet others from different backgrounds and segregating people identifies those from the 'other' community negatively as being different.

> Because there's no point making you feel different and being put in separate places – just put them together. Some ignorant people wouldn't want to but it wouldn't bother me to be put in a mixed Protestant and Catholic school.
> *(17-year-old female – foster care)*

> Mixed – because if it's one religion from you're five until you're eighteen you've no chance of meeting others or learning about others because you're in schools six hours a day of your life.
> *(16-year-old female – NIMMA)*

> Mix – because it shouldn't matter what religion you are. You should be friends with everyone.
> *(14-year-old female – foster care)*

> Extern was mixed and it wasn't violent. It keeps you off the streets and you get to know all of them and there's no fights.
> *(14-year-old male – residential care)*

Children also explained that at social clubs people could choose whether or not to attend and people's religious identity would not be as evident because they would not be wearing uniforms. Children who were in favour of mixed housing suggested this would make more areas safe for everyone, lessen sectarian tension and increase mutual understanding.

> Mix – because you can't feel comfortable when it's segregated because there's that many fights. You need to be integrated to feel safe in both areas. Now you stand out in each area and if you're walking towards an area like through a Catholic area heading towards a Protestant area they know where you're going and they target you. It's the same if you're on a bus going that direction the Catholics stone it even though there's Catholics on it and children that could get hurt.
> *(21-year-old female – leaving care)*

In contrast, although other children generally felt that sectarian or religious divisions in community areas were negative, they suggested segregation was preferable to avoid the likelihood of sectarian tension or violence:

> It depends if they're non-sectarian but here I think they should stay together because there is sectarian people and there would be too many fights, so stay together to be safer.
> *(14-year-old female – home on Care Order)*

> Stay together – because I was at a mixed school and they were killing each other and fighting away with each other.
> *(12-year-old male – residential care)*

> It's really hard. The estate could be wrecked if it was mixed. If you put them together they would never learn anything. There'd just be riots about things like stealing flags. Stay together for peace.
> *(15-year-old female – child in need)*

Indeed, several children who were in favour of integration also expressed concern about the possibility of violence and conflict:

> Housing would be the most difficult because rows would start and then people would start moving out.
> *(NIMMA, focus group)*

> Mix. No not really – sort of. On Catholic days and Protestant days people would have their windows put through.
> *(14-year-old female – child in need)*

Comments children made about belonging in their community area suggests that, despite sectarian tensions, living in segregated communities offered them a stronger community identity:

> I would like to live in a mixed area but they're only in the country and even if you could get out there you wouldn't be accepted because you're a city person. I feel more comfortable in Protestant areas than Catholic areas because in Catholic areas there's more hoods and joyriding. Catholics go on as if they're like black people. Protestants aren't as bad that way but they're different. Protestants are more bigoted than Catholics. Like Protestants wouldn't want a Catholic to be walking up their road even but Catholics wouldn't care if Protestants are walking on their road.
> *(21-year-old female – leaving care)*

> It's good. It teaches you about everybody else in the area. Everywhere surrounding us is Catholics and we're in the centre. But there's a lot of conflict here and riots and my friend's death. Everyone was traumatised by the riots.
> *(15-year-old female – foster care)*

Summary

Living in segregated areas and attending segregated clubs and schools restricted opportunities for children to mix with peers from both religious backgrounds. It also increased pressure on cross-community children to keep their dual identity secret or conform to the dominant religion. Overall, children did not feel that religion was an important factor in their relationships with peers and the majority of cross-community children were in favour of integrated education, social spaces and housing areas. However, children were acutely aware of other people's attitudes towards cross-community families and the danger of sectarian conflict or violence.

5. Social work and other support services for cross-community families

This chapter explores the provision of social work and other support services for cross-community families such as assistance from the Northern Ireland Housing Executive (NIHE). Social workers' views on the needs of cross-community children and the services they provided to meet the needs of cross-community families are discussed. The chapter also reports parental views on social work services and levels of support services available to cross-community families living in Northern Ireland.

Social workers' perceptions of the needs of cross-community children

Interestingly, more than half of field social workers (11 out of 21) suggested that cross-community children did not have any particular needs. These social workers felt that all children had the same needs, relating to parental background, education and health.

Field social workers (10 out of 21) who felt cross-community children did face particular issues identified their key needs as: developing self-identity, accessing integrated services, maintaining contact with both sides of their family, learning about both religious and cultural backgrounds, and dealing with sectarianism. The quotations below illustrate typical comments from these social workers:

> I suppose it is wanting to belong more to one section of the community than the other, where they see themselves belonging. Then it is trying to get themselves accepted in that particular part of the community if they are cross-religion. I worked with a family in [area], being predominantly Protestant and one particular wee fellow

> whose father was Catholic – this was continuously held up to him and it was a huge issue about the fact that the Daddy was Catholic because he wanted to be seen to be with the Protestant gangs … and he wanted to be accepted by them. He didn't want anybody knowing that his father was actually a Catholic and it was very, very difficult for him.
> *(Field Social Worker)*

> They need to know about their cultures and their backgrounds and how to deal with the questions they get asked and are faced with. Sectarianism and the process of what is said about the other parent and stereotypes. How they fit in with sectarianism here and paramilitary groups which is actually targeting teenagers … Schools, where they live and the influence of environment will all impact on which religion they will choose … they may experience sectarianism from a very young age.
> *(Field Social Worker)*

> I would say to feel that they've got equal rights to all the community supports and resources. And there is a problem, depending on where the child lives, as to what services they can access, what priority they're giving to some services. I guess as well they would need to feel that they would be accepted within those services and not stigmatised and not singled out as being different and … it's difficult to find public housing in a non-affiliated area or a non-sectarian area.
> *(Field Social Worker)*

All of the five principal social workers also recognised the particular needs of cross-community children, however, they suggested that social workers did not seriously consider their experiences and needs.

> These cross-community children are more likely to be looked after because the informal network is not maintained. One person has left the fold and is still outside the fold and there is no informal support when they hit bad times and there are less extended ties routinely and ordinarily.
> *(Principal Social Worker)*

> I think that this is an area that by and large is neglected from the point of view of policy ... and we have to incorporate that within the planning processes that exist and provide training for staff and for carers. I think it's an area that needs to be improved ... I think children from cross-community families can be confused about who they are and what they are in a sense, and sometimes it can cause relationship difficulties ... Children have issues at school especially and wouldn't tell their friends or at school that they are from a cross-community background. So there is pressure to keep secrets at school and the family, the neighbourhood or youth clubs. They will have to avoid being targeted, ostracised or bullied from peers. People really do assume and even in my work some social workers have attitudes about mixed marriages. One meeting I had with a social worker who was discussing a case involving a mixed marriage breakdown and said 'oh that's what happens to these mixed marriages'. Children from cross-community relationships can be perceived as different and you have to be able to talk to children about this ... I do appreciate the more and more I think of this that there are certainly more issues involved there that really do require more thought.
> ***(Principal Social Worker)***

Five of the six parents contacted through NIMMA were involved in offering advice or information for other parents in mixed marriages who had contacted NIMMA. Based on their own experiences and listening to other parents in mixed marriages, they identified the key needs of cross-community children as: forming an identity, coping with being treated differently, meeting other cross-community children and being able to talk openly about being cross-community.

> Identity is the biggest one I think. Teachers and parents need to support them and they need to be able to engage with cross-community life.
> ***(Mother, NIMMA)***

They also felt parents of cross-community children needed information and advice on how to deal with important issues including: arranging ceremonies such as marriage and baptism, dealing with opposing families, accessing safe and neutral housing, and promoting the identity needs of their family. They emphasised that meeting other cross-community families is very helpful for those who need support and information from others who have similar experiences.

> Marriage and baptisms. How are you going to do a baptism, now you can have children jointly baptised and it's important for family from the Protestants and Catholics in the other church to feel that it's validated like by grannies and aunties and cousins. Another issue is decisions about education because you can hide up until that ... Parents need to give their children the language and courage they will need to empower them and as such some of these people have been pioneers but family relationships can become really twisted with parents not wanting to meet their children and lots of things like that.
> *(Mother, NIMMA)*

Safe housing comes into it really. Supportive family and friends. And supportive clergy is important. And really we're in such a divided society it's easy to feel alienated from the political part of it and I think probably what's really needed to get is a sense where others are so there is an identity for people who are cross-community ... you know, kids are going to be asked on forms do they belong to the Protestant or Catholic community, you know, they should have both and understand both, but there isn't a both there.
(Mother, NIMMA)

Anti-discriminatory and anti-sectarian policies

Since social workers felt that the impact of sectarianism and unequal access to neutral services were central to the needs of cross-community children it was important to explore how anti-discriminatory and anti-sectarian policies translated into practice. However, more than two thirds of social workers were unaware of specific anti-discriminatory or anti-sectarian policies:

> No training or policies that I am aware of. Although often social workers come up against it. It wasn't even part of the course when I qualified.
> *(Field Social Worker)*

Some of these social workers suggested that it is more important that anti-discrimination and anti-sectarianism were viewed as core social work values rather than specific policies:

> I don't really think about legislation but practice ... It's built into our training, not policy, but values I base my practice on – to treat everybody fairly and recognise everyone has difficulties and work with them.
> *(Residential Social Worker)*

Principal social workers also noted, that although there were no specific Trust policies for anti-discriminatory or anti-sectarian practice, there was an expectation that this was an integral part of their everyday professional practice. They also emphasised that further training for social work staff was required to address anti-sectarian issues and fulfil current legislative requirements.

> There probably aren't any specific anti-discrimination policies but social workers and social work ethics is very much anti-discriminatory ... I don't think it's addressed specifically as such but it's inherent throughout it. Certainly the ethos of the whole Trust is anti-sectarian, I mean we deal with Catholic and Protestant families in a very similar way ... So from the code of ethics, the Northern Ireland Social Care Council and social work as a profession certainly promotes anti-discriminatory practice and anti-sectarian practice.
> *(Principal Social Worker)*

> I suppose we just have that the Trust is bound by our equality legislation and all of our policies are equality impact assessed on religion so that we do not discriminate against anybody in our services ... I think probably for most social workers it's part of their training basically. The social workers must be able to demonstrate anti-discriminatory practice ... To what extent staff think about the issue I don't know and I think there is a struggle there, because the whole issue of anti-sectarianism is actually identified as a training issue for staff. I

think we were looking at how exactly we were to undertake this kind of training for staff and what exactly it meant because it is an issue that probably over the years people have tended to put to one side … it's been a neglected area really because it's just ignored, leave it to others and don't get into it because to get into it results in raising difficult issues for people. But it's not specific to social care either, it's true all over including the broader health service.
(Principal Social Worker)

Parental perspectives on social work services

None of the parents of children in need or looked after children felt that being cross-community was the main reason why they were in contact with social services. Parents of children in need explained the reasons for their contact with social services were to address problems related to inadequate support systems, children's challenging behaviour, domestic violence, mental illness or alcohol addiction. Parents of looked after children suggested the reasons their children were looked after were related to mental illness, neglect, physical abuse, children's challenging behaviour or alcohol addiction. Figure 5.1 shows the reasons cited in case files for children in this study being looked after.

Figure 5.1 Reasons cross-community children are looked after

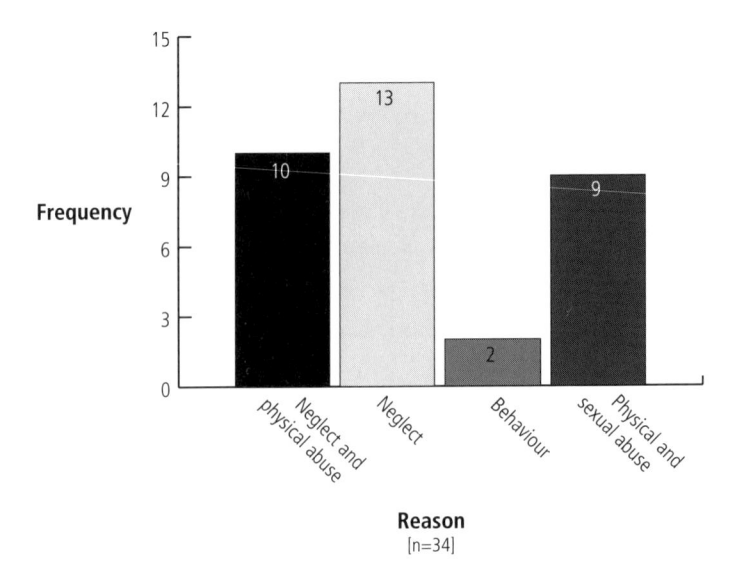

Reason	Frequency
Neglect and physical abuse	10
Neglect	13
Behaviour	2
Physical and sexual abuse	9

[n=34]

Although parents did not feel being cross-community was the main reason why their children became looked after, they did acknowledge the negative impact of stressors that only cross-community families experience. For example, one parent explained that when she began to experience problems she found it difficult to ask for support because being ostracised by her family had forced her to try to cope independently for so long:

> I can't blame the Trust. It was my own pride. I couldn't cope and I let it get out of hand. I wouldn't ask and it was the same as my marriage, I wouldn't ask for help.
> *(Mother of looked after child)*

Half of the parents of children in need who were experiencing problems at home felt that support services could be improved. These parents were dissatisfied that responses from social services failed to adequately address problems they were experiencing such as dealing with paramilitary threats, children's challenging behaviour or insufficient local services for their children. Some of these parents felt their social worker had little understanding of the problems families experienced, shared inaccurate information with other professionals or were overly intrusive in their family's life:

> I don't like them. They offered services but I wouldn't take them. I find them degrading and they have their mind made up from the start so you're up against it. [husband] was an alcoholic and they had no understanding of alcoholism as an illness … Social workers are invasive on family life. For example, one time we found out they had it on file for a case conference that the schools and everything were reading that I had an affair and it was untrue and when I confronted them with it they then admitted it was a mistake but sure everyone had read it … You can't be soft with them. I know families who are tortured by social services.
> *(Mother of child in need)*

The remaining parents of children in need were happy with levels of support services they received from social services. These parents felt their social worker was a positive support for their family and provided flexible practical and emotional assistance:

> He was a very good support and he tried his best to help us. He gave us a break with respite and would have even took them out himself to give us a break. There was Extern every day for two to three hours to diffuse tension at home. Respite, family centre and a family support worker that took him to teach him to wash and tidy his room. The social worker would've called once or twice a week … up to the house.
> *(Father of child in need)*

Only a quarter of parents of looked after children were satisfied with the levels of support services they had received and almost all of the parents of looked after children would have liked more support when they first had contact with social services.

> They were very bad. After their mother died I went back to work … I had looked after her for a long time when she was ill. No one took my feelings into account … I was broke and I had to work and pay childcare. My job was on building sites so I was doing long hours and it wasn't structured enough for me to be home to collect the kids from childcare. I got no help because I was a man. I was trying to cope but we had no support. The cost of the children being in care was more than what I wanted to help me pay childcare during the day when I was at work ... If I had had that money at that time I might've been able to keep them.
> *(Father of looked after child)*

> Looking back I had no support whatsoever. Maybe if I had things would have been different. I had nothing from the social worker – only complaints.
> *(Mother of looked after child)*

> They never really gave you a chance, they just took the weens … I would've liked more support with a second chance.
> *(Mother of looked after child)*

Four parents of looked after children were particularly unhappy about the lack of information that social workers provided about their child's life after they became looked after.

> What I'm saying is that the one thing was I wasn't informed when things were happening in his life – so that's been a problem. They tell me absolutely nothing.
> *(Mother of looked after child)*

> I would like more comeback on placements. They give you no feedback. I don't know why I'm not allowed overnight stays with him.
> *(Mother of looked after child)*

Interestingly, two parents of looked after children had both negative and positive experiences of contact with social services:

> Well basically what they told me I was to stay away from his daddy because it was a very violent relationship. Plus I had a drink problem as well as his daddy and because I had contact with him that was it. I'm not with that Trust any more now, I'm with a different Trust at the moment. And they are extremely helpful. A thousand times better. I get a lot of services from this Trust. They've been really helpful … they arranged for family support worker to help with light housework, they arranged for a home help, they've arranged for the child minding services and they pay for it. I had postnatal depression … and ended up in hospital for three weeks. They arranged for foster care for the two of them. Once I started getting back on my feet after the depression they arranged for me for a family centre to reunite us together.
> *Interviewer: And would you have liked to have access to those sorts of services earlier?*
> Yes, because I didn't know all those sorts of services were available. I would have used them, you know, but I was never told about anything. If I'd had the family support and the services I'm getting now the chances are, I mean me and [looked after child] could have been back together, you know, before it went on that long…
> *(Mother of looked after child)*

> Social workers that came didn't understand and they had no experience of children or marriage to realise the pressures we were under. [Current social worker] was the first social worker who understood because she is married with

> children. Her attitude and the way she goes on so bubbly – you know she comes in here and makes herself at home and she talks to our children and takes them out. The boys are dying about her. She is a good social worker.
> *(Father of looked after child)*

Dissatisfied parents identified other support services that would have been useful for their family and may have prevented their children becoming looked after. These included respite care, childcare provision, anger management, access to social activities and increased supports within their own communities:

> I voluntarily gave the children into care. I wish they had the things I have now like time out and respite. That would've been better but they thought it wasn't appropriate so they were placed in care. Once they were in the care setting it was totally impossible to bring them back. And it causes problems when they do come back because they give them so much and then they expect so much all the time like money and new clothes.
> *(Mother of looked after child)*

> I wanted someone there for me - anybody there. And somewhere for the weens to go like a big play park. There was total demand on me in the summer and the schemes were too expensive – it would have helped us a lot.
> *(Mother of looked after child)*

> Well it would have been nice to have the family behind me. People to give good advice the odd time – what to do and what not to do. If I was doing something wrong, you know, if I wasn't bringing up the child right, advise like what if you did it this way it would work better, be easier, things like that. Maybe [looked after son] would still be here.
> *(Mother of looked after child)*

Parents of children in need and parents from NIMMA also identified services that would ensure better support for cross-community families. In addition to those mentioned by parents of looked after children, these included access to cross-community activities and family therapy.

> In this area the community don't do anything for themselves. They only fight among each other and do nothing for the young ones.
> *(Mother of child in need)*

> Housing because so much of that is segregated. Education because it is also mainly segregated and causes so much labelling. Structures need to change to accommodate the whole community here. There also needs to be more integrated social clubs and integrated schools are pioneering that but safety is a big issue. They could train social workers because they are widely ignorant and trainers could be trained and that's not just for social workers but also other professionals.
> *(Mother, NIMMA)*

> There should be services for people who find it difficult to talk about things. An outsider doing family therapy. You know someone from outside the family with a special interest in mixed marriages. It's really all about making decisions together to suit everyone and those extra decisions which involve emotions of the wider family.
> *(Mother, NIMMA)*

The majority of social workers also felt there were inadequate services provided for cross-community families. This was because of the general lack of services available for all children, segregated service provision and the impact of living in a sectarian environment. Social workers felt that services should become more integrated and provide support across communities so all families could access them. They also suggested that all children should have more opportunities to participate in cross-community activities to increase understanding and tolerance of religious and cultural diversity.

> I definitely don't think there is enough from the cross-community youth clubs and it has become very polarised and kids get streetwise … I suppose it's just how little there really is in terms of services out there to help kids understand each other's customs. There is so little and an awful lot of the work and the change and development of young people must come from the carers, teachers, parents, or residential social workers or education plays a huge part.
> *(Residential Social Worker)*

> Housing ... all other estates have paramilitary elements
> within it and ... it's not safe for those families. Access to
> services can be a problem for those families as well,
> especially cross-community groups.
> **(Field Social Worker)**

> I don't think there's enough services in general and I think
> those children are just forgotten about really to be honest.
> I suppose it's just a shame ... They're just forgotten about
> really ... looking at the referring agents it looks that way,
> you've got to be in one box or the other.
> **(Field Social Worker)**

Two principal social workers felt there were adequate services for cross-community families because they assumed cross-community children usually affiliated with one religious identity or lived in neutral areas:

> I suppose our own services are open to anybody from any
> background, although ... in our society we have where some
> areas and estates that maybe get it on the basis of one
> particular religious community or another and I suspect
> children from cross-community backgrounds probably don't
> live in those areas ... that they live in communities where there
> are some degree of mixing as opposed to one or the other.
> **(Principal Social Worker)**

However, others agreed that accessible support services for children, including cross-community children, needed to be further developed in their Trust areas.

> I think we have to develop our portfolio of support services
> throughout the area ... this Trust has got a major urban
> situation because it's segregated so we need to make sure
> that we've got services that both communities can avail
> [themselves] of ... so it's not just a matter of trying to get it
> close geographically, it's trying to make sure that they're
> culturally sensitive.
> **(Principal Social Worker)**

Other support services

Families and social workers also discussed the availability of support from other services. These were assistance with housing from the Housing Executive and services from voluntary organisations, including NIMMA.

One parent from NIMMA, three of the parents of children in need and almost half of the parents of looked after children had accessed assistance with housing. Only two parents were satisfied with the support they had received from the Housing Executive and this was because they had been placed in a safe, mixed area. All of the remaining parents were unhappy with support they had received from the Housing Executive. This was because the Housing Executive had re-housed families in segregated areas that placed their family at risk or responded slowly to immediate housing needs.

> The communication with the housing executives, absolutely abysmal, the letters I poured my heart out to the manager and they were not replying to it, I was told misinformation, offered a house where a Catholic family had been intimidated out of, and it was boarded up … but it was very unpleasant and I waited eight weeks to be offered something … It was really awful and I'm sure the housing executive has a hard job, but there's nothing. What really worried me about the Housing Executive that there are no free houses in mixed estates so the best you can do is do it privately … It was really a disgrace.
> **(Mother, NIMMA)**

> The Housing Executive … would save houses in mixed areas and reserve places for mixed marriages in NI but there's never any available.
> **(Father, NIMMA)**

Only three of the parents of children in need and three of the parents of looked after children received services from voluntary organisations. These organisations were Women's Aid, Alcoholics Anonymous, Gingerbread, Newpin, Homestart, Bryson House, local women's centres, and parent and toddler groups. These parents were satisfied with the range of services from these organisations and felt they provided valuable support for their family. Interestingly, none of the parents of children in need or children looked after had accessed NIMMA services. Overall, parents emphasised the importance of locating support groups from voluntary organisations in local areas that are safely accessible for cross-community families.

Parents from NIMMA who did receive support from that organisation or who worked for NIMMA provided some insight into the mutual support service they provided. NIMMA mainly provided information and advice and offered an opportunity to meet with other cross-community families. Members of NIMMA received support services and also provided advice and support for other families. NIMMA also educated and liaised with other organisations who could support people in cross-community relationships, such as clerical groups, integrated schools or pre-marriage counselling groups. Unfortunately, these external agencies did not include social services or the Housing Executive:

> We have offered it to other courses like social work and housing but it's too controversial and a hundred per cent ignored it.
> *(Father, NIMMA)*

Parents enjoyed meeting other cross-community families at NIMMA and learning from the experiences of others on matters such as deciding about children's religious upbringing or dealing with family relatives:

> I don't think we were looking overtly for support but the fact we belonged to the group was a comfort and ... you are actually getting support because you are with like-minded people and you can talk very openly and you are very free.
> *(Father, NIMMA)*

> I suppose it's an opportunity to find families who are at different levels, different stages, you know. My children are very young and ... I'd just love to talk to teenagers to see their experiences and to see if there's anything they feel that we could do that could make any difference for our children. I think one of the big things that I want was exploring experiences that people have already been there. We might make the same decisions anyway, but at least we would know more. Their children are older than ours at the next stage.
> *(Mother, NIMMA)*

However, three of the parents in contact with NIMMA identified ways in which this service could be further developed. Most of the couples accessing this service were married. One parent felt that this excluded many others who are not married but are in cross-community relationships and experience similar difficulties. Another parent suggested that since NIMMA only had a base in Belfast it was inaccessible for people from other areas of Northern Ireland to become fully involved as members. One parent recommended that NIMMA required additional funding to extend to other areas of Northern Ireland, especially more rural areas.

Summary

More than half of all social workers interviewed believed that cross-community children did not have any significant needs or experiences. This was in contrast to the range of issues that parents and other social workers reported that these children faced in their daily lives. The majority of parents did not feel that being cross-community was the main reason for their contact with social services or their children becoming looked after. However, they did acknowledge that additional pressures on cross-community families adds to their stress and decreases their access to informal support systems when they begin to experience problems. Half of the parents of children in need and three quarters of the parents of looked after children were dissatisfied with the support services available to them when they first experienced difficulties. Families required more accessible support services based in local communities and neutral, safe areas. Support services that did exist, such as NIMMA, also needed to be further developed to make them accessible to more families.

The impact of sectarianism and living in a predominantly segregated society had a detrimental impact on the provision of social work and other support services. However, two thirds of social workers were unaware of anti-discriminatory or anti-sectarian policies related to their work. Instead, social workers suggested anti-discrimination and anti-sectarianism were integral parts of the ethical foundation of the social work profession. This created space for individual social workers to adopt their own approaches in their daily work; however, this also meant that many social workers ignored issues relating to sectarianism. Indeed, principal social workers recognised that dealing with sectarianism was a very difficult aspect of social work practice.

6. Meeting the needs of cross-community children who are looked after

This chapter discusses how social workers meet the particular needs of cross-community children who are looked after. It looks first at the challenges for social workers in terms of identifying and recording children's religious identity, including difficulties related to consulting children and their parents about religious upbringing. Issues that arise when seeking a placement for cross-community children are also identified, including specific issues for children living in residential care. Finally, the key factors influencing children's contact with family members are discussed.

Identifying child's religious identity

Social workers seeking to meet the needs of children must first of all identify their needs. Therefore, it was necessary to investigate how social workers identified and recorded the religious and cultural needs of looked after children. Social workers explained they would identify children's religious background by consulting their files or asking the child's family and other professionals. However, many social workers noted that records of children's religious identity often did not provide any detail.

> That's an area that really needs to be pushed and I think half the time is just not filled in any detail and religion isn't seen as the big picture sometimes when a child is in a situation where they have been abused ... so it can kind of get lost in all of that and the Trust it is so understaffed at the moment so you can very easily get lost.
> **(Residential Social Worker)**

Overall, more than half of the social workers (18 out of 31) felt that records of cross-community children's religious or cultural identity were often incomplete and inaccurate. They suggested this could be because the information was not available, staff did not have time to keep their records up-to-date or other issues were prioritised:

> They're very poor. There are huge gaps and whole portions of children's lives are missing. That's an ongoing problem and we are not overcoming it. Maybe information is not available or it's not sought or is not given to us by the other social workers or maybe families. That could be because they're genuinely too busy or don't want to pre-judge the child or the situation.
> ***(Residential Social Worker)***

> Very under-developed. It reflects the whole of Northern Ireland scenario of don't mention it. It's something that has been sidestepped ... We don't have any training on it. If it's known it will be filled in but it will be scant because we don't think about it.
> ***(Residential Social Worker)***

> From my own experience it's not really that accurate. I suppose at times just assumptions are made because we are focused on other issues that are really important, how healthy is the child, how are they interacting with their foster family, contact with their natural family, all these are big and important issues. It's a lot to do with the social workers not having time as well to keep records and files up to date because you can't do everything, that sort of takes precedence.
> ***(Field Social Worker)***

Social workers claimed that children's religious and cultural identity should be recorded on initial referral forms, essential information records for all looked after children and admission forms for all children entering residential care. However, several social workers claimed that for children from cross-community backgrounds and children placed in care in an emergency this information was often not known. Social workers who suggested records were accurate explained it was part of their statutory duty to ascertain that information and record it on file and in Looked After Children (LAC) forms. However, even principal social workers were aware that records may not always be accurate or complete and planned to address this through internal auditing, staff training and awareness raising.

> We need to sharpen up on this and I think internal audits will pick up on what is not documented. Social workers don't like this but if it's not right there's a difficulty. They are only looking at the bits that really need to be covered and there's not enough emphasis on the consequences for not filling it in. We need to raise awareness that policies exist and get people talking about it. Seniors need to have a meeting with team leaders and talk about the implications with teams and raise consciousness because no importance is attached to it and how it fits with preoccupations with risk so we need to be selling it.
> *(Principal Social Worker)*

Indeed, Figure 6.1 shows that more than half of all the social workers made assumptions about the religious identity of children when they became looked after.

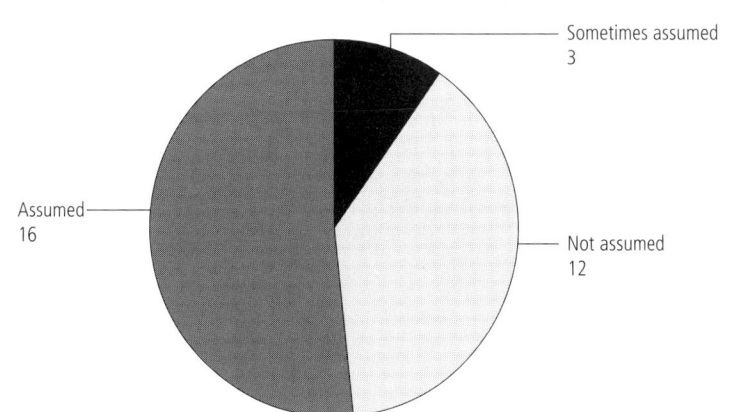

Figure 6.1 Social workers assume children's religious identity

- Assumed 16
- Sometimes assumed 3
- Not assumed 12

Surprisingly, eight of these social workers indicated that it was appropriate to make assumptions about children's religious background. When cross-community children first came to the attention of social services, most social workers assumed that they were raised in one religious faith rather than both.

These assumptions were usually based on the school they attended, their name or where they lived.

> I think when we get referrals and to be honest a lot of the time it's see what you make of the child, and if it's a Catholic or Protestant school you might assume that the child is Protestant or Catholic, and when you went to an area and it was Catholic or Protestant area you might then assume that they are Catholic or Protestant. You would look at things like their name as well. And to be honest, I don't think I've ever gone out to a family and said 'What religion are you?' It's probably not very good practice but I think that's my experience that you would guess what religion they are. People are too scared to ask. I think it can be insulting, especially in Northern Ireland regarding religion. I think another reason too might be that it should be so obvious what religion they are that you shouldn't have to ask and when you do ask you might feel stupid saying 'What religion are you?'
> *(Field Social Worker)*

When religious upbringing was not decided, social workers promoted the religious identity of the dominant parent or identified the religious persuasion of children by their attendance at segregated schools. This meant that most social workers had not considered cross-community children as having a mixed identity.

> If their parents are bringing them up as Protestants you make sure that there's a church that they can go to … then it would depend on really the schools that they go to … I don't think it's a burning issue but they would be forced to really choose. I think it's very difficult for a child who doesn't chose.
> *(Field Social Worker)*

> It's at the back of your mind. It wouldn't be at the forefront … we don't really promote cross-community, it's more the dominant religion.
> *(Field Social Worker)*

Consulting family members about children's religious and cultural identity

All of the social workers involved in this study agreed they would consult family members about looked after children's religious and cultural upbringing. These family members were usually parents, however sometimes external family members, such as grandparents or aunts, were involved if they played a significant role in the child's life. However the great majority of social workers (25 out of 31) said there were major challenges in consulting families about religion and culture. The small minority of social workers who felt there were no significant challenges related this to information and explained that collecting this information was an essential part of care planning and should not raise any particular challenges if it is approached sensitively with family members.

> I think it is again one of those things if you approach it sensibly and say 'We are obviously planning for a full care plan for your child' and 'What are your views on' so the parents are included and involved in our process that makes everything easier.
> *(Field Social Worker)*

> It is essential information but we don't make a mountain of it – it's just a question.
> *(Field Social Worker)*

However, there were individual cases when these social workers also admitted they were unsure if parents had been actively involved in decisions about their child's religious and cultural upbringing. The social worker quoted below is describing a case where the mother informed the researcher she had no input into decisions about the religious and cultural upbringing of her children.

> With our partnership we have kept his mother very well informed about his needs and how we are responding to those needs.
> *Interviewer: And agreed then that he is Protestant?*
> Certainly, currently face to face relations that I have with her, she is aware of the fact that he's going to continue possibly the Protestant education system and she's not disagreeing with it.

> *Interviewer: Has she specified any particular type of Protestant faith that she wants him brought up in like Presbyterian or Church of Ireland?*
> I've never asked her outright. She's never been asked – it wasn't a subject for discussion.
> *(Field Social Worker)*

The majority of social workers had experienced particular challenges related to consulting family members about their child's religious and cultural upbringing. Interviews indicated there were three reasons for this: they found it difficult to consult parents or children who held very strong religious or political beliefs; families felt social workers were being judgemental by asking about their religion; or parents made biased assumptions about social workers' religious background. Consultation was also challenging when children and parents disagreed, when parents disagreed with each other or when parents had not decided about the child's religious upbringing.

> I imagine some people might be embarrassed about it, because of the society we live in. Certainly mixed marriages in certain parts of society are frowned upon to the point where they are almost a taboo subject. I imagine a challenge could be the fact that the parents have split, separated, divorced. If we as social work carers are telling one of the respective parents that we have to tolerate both sides of the child's background, one parent may react in a hostile way because they've fallen back into their original community. They are actually responding in their own sectarian ways.
> *(Residential Social Worker)*

> People get very fiery about religion like going to Mass or church. Suddenly religion becomes a big issue and it is one of the main questions if they're in foster care ... It comes back to sectarianism and politics in Northern Ireland that turns people into two-eyed monsters.
> *(Field Social Worker)*

> It is such a sensitive issue I think sometimes parents feel you are passing judgement on them and I think it would be very difficult to say 'No I don't particularly wish for my child to attend a religious ceremony once a week' ... because they

> might feel that reflects on their opinion of their level of upbringing or morality or something like that. I would find it difficult to ask a parent in the way that I felt they wouldn't interpret it as being judgemental. I'm just terrified of offending somebody by saying the wrong thing.
> *(Field Social Worker)*

These social workers described feeling awkward and uncomfortable about asking questions about families' religious backgrounds and recognised that this was a very sensitive and private issue for families and professionals within a divided society:

> Sometimes I feel uneasy about it because with some people it is a touchy subject. At the end of the day because I have no axe to grind so there's nothing in it personally … but to a lot of people it is a phenomenal subject.
> *(Field Social Worker)*

> It annoys me having to ask people and it's more to do with Northern Ireland. It immediately gets people's suspicions up and some feel that will affect the services they get and some people feel they could be discriminated against.
> *(Field Social Worker)*

Therefore, some social workers suggested that questions about religious identity would be asked later when they had developed a closer working relationship with the family.

Several social workers believed that recording information on children's religious and cultural identity was not always necessary:

> Where we live does recording religious background make things any better or worse? And you could argue that it doesn't get any better and it doesn't get any worse. My own personal opinion is religion is responsible for ninety-nine per cent if not a hundred per cent of the upset in the world today. It doesn't matter what procedures or policies you get they are only effective when the people are prepared to work with you; you can only do your best.
> *(Field Social Worker)*

> I think there's too much information held on the children and what that's being used for and why it's being used. I think that when children come into care, we collate all the information about them, for instance if they're identified as a Protestant then we have all sorts of issues about them going to church or them, going to their ceremonies and what's meeting their needs and what's not meeting their needs. And I think for a lot of children they may be pushed into that.
> *(Field Social Worker)*

Principal social workers confirmed that recording children's religious background is part of the essential information required for children who are looked after. They also recognised that staff must approach the subject of religion sensitively at an appropriate time and suggested that some social workers may assume religious identity rather than ask parents or children. Principal social workers acknowledged that social workers do not have any guidance on how they should ask families about religious identity, however they still expected them to collect that information and explain to parents that it would assist care planning for their child.

> I think social workers are anxious about asking the obvious. There are no procedures and guidelines but there is an assumption that you would ask. If we had a hostile parent from a strong community background we wouldn't ask if we are putting ourselves at risk or there is a potential for violence. In a recent review we did notice there were blanks or not applicables written for those sections so we need to point out to our staff that that needs to be completed. Social workers need to explain to families why we need to know and explain if it is not recorded why it is not.
> *(Principal Social Worker)*

Principal social workers also recognised that although forms for looked after children request information on their religious and cultural background, they usually did not provide detail for children from cross-community backgrounds and records may not be accurate. Two principal social workers recommended that, rather than offering limited choices by ticking boxes, forms should allow more space to add comments that facilitate more effective care planning.

> We did an audit of our essential information records ... to try and re-emphasise the need for information gathering for the process of planning. So it wasn't just tick this box, it was more to try and get the understanding if you haven't got that information how can you plan, you know, it's a living breathing process as opposed to just a tick box thing.
> *(Principal Social Worker)*

> Staff have had a difficulty about particularly religion, of asking the question about that. So what has happened is that it is left blank or they assume ethnicity and don't ask about religion. Now when we identify the background it would probably be the religious background as stated by the carer and it would generally be one or the other, it would not probably show that this may be a cross-community family. So it is not possible to identify from it unless we were told ... And I asked the systems manager to print out the number of cases where there was nothing entered, and there was quite a number ... but that should be known ... part of that is to do with workload issues, and just maybe cutting corners basically... and a lot of those forms are based on textbook tick box schemes ... I suppose there are opportunities to indicate differences all the way on the forms ... but they've not always been taken and again that maybe linked round to what extent we see the religious issues as being an important one in comparison to other areas about health, contact names, behaviour ...
> *(Principal Social Worker)*

Consulting children about their religious and cultural identity

Of the 31 social workers interviewed, 18 suggested they also consulted children about their religious and cultural upbringing. However, their comments revealed that most of these social workers usually only consulted children about attendance at church services.

> I think they're actively asked about attendance and it's part of our role to recognise their cultural needs but you ask yourself 'Are you just asking the question or are you genuinely looking to try and promote it?'
> **(Residential Social Worker)**

Additionally, 11 social workers claimed they only consulted older children or young people.

> Depends on the age of the child, but certainly it's something they would talk to a child of well eleven or twelve onwards. I would talk too about their thoughts and feelings about their religion and their own culture and how they keep their own identity, but prior to that, really to be honest I would see religion as a secondary thing for the younger ones. You know, once I had established what schools they're going to and where they're going on Sunday. But for the older child I suppose it is because they're facing bigger issues.
> **(Residential Social Worker)**

Other social workers admitted children were not generally consulted about this:

> The paramount principle in the Children's Order is not carried through in this area and they're not usually consulted.
> **(Residential Social Worker)**

Two thirds of all the social workers felt there were particular challenges related to consulting children about their religious and cultural identity. The main challenges were dealing with children's experience of sectarianism, being able to provide comprehensive and unbiased information about religion and culture, discussing with children how their views on religion are connected with their feelings for each parent and dealing with parents' and children's conflicting views.

> There's difficulty both if you're from a different religion as a young person, but equally there's challenges if you're from the same religion as the young person because if I was talking to a Catholic child I can relate to that in a way by asking, you know, 'What happens in that? What does that mean?' And if I'm talking to a Protestant child and there's a certain amount of self disclosure but there's also the fear then of not being bigoted or anti-Catholic. And it's about

making sure that you're talking about equality. Some of the young people we talk to or work with would be very loyal so when you're talking to a child you want to relate to the child but also you don't want to condone any sectarianism or militancy … but it may be easier if you don't have very strong views either way.
(Residential Social Worker)

Kids often rebel against family members if they are quite staunch or they had bad experiences especially if they're cross-community ... which one do they choose? And that can be linked to their feelings for a parent. This child was caught vandalising a Catholic school and he has a Union Jack and plays Loyalist music and there are identity issues there and that's probably related to his mum. I haven't talked to him about that.
(Field Social Worker)

It could be a bit sort of daunting to sit down and talk to children about anything like cultural background. Say for example they were brought up with a Loyalist family it could be difficult. I would find it quite difficult sitting there talking about religion. I would be worried about what sort of issues they would bring up, maybe how we deal with them issues.
(Field Social Worker)

The remaining one third of social workers felt there were no particular challenges because they would be open and honest in discussions about religion with children and seek information and advice from others if necessary.

Looked after placements for cross-community children

Social workers outlined six key issues they considered when they sought a placement for looked after cross-community children:

- maintaining the religious upbringing children had at home, especially church attendance
- flexibility of carers to facilitate promotion of child's mixed religious and cultural needs

- availability of cross-community carers
- location of placement in a neutral area
- availability of suitable local social and cultural activities for the child
- access to appropriate schools.

However, some social workers emphasised that they sought a safe placement first and foremost so consideration of other issues was secondary.

> To be honest when you're looking for a placement first of all you're looking for a placement. You're looking at the child not religion ... So our priority is just to get a placement.
> *(Field Social Worker)*

> Sometimes you've got children in such direst states out here that quite honestly you wouldn't bother about religion.
> *(Field Social Worker)*

All of the principal social workers and social workers agreed that there was a shortage of placements available for looked after children in general and especially an insufficient diversity to match the religious needs of cross-community children. Therefore, some social workers emphasised that when they were seeking placements for these children they focused on the flexibility and willingness of carers to meet their diverse religious and cultural needs.

> It's not always possible to place a child in a family of same religion but it is possible to place children with a family who are sensitive to the needs of the child and promoting their needs. They would find a way around meeting needs of child with a different religion like taking them to ceremonies.
> *(Field Social Worker)*

Principal social workers suggested there was a general lack of foster care provision despite recent recruitment drives. Social workers offered three possible reasons for this: the demands on foster carers have changed as children's needs have become more complex; societal structures have changed as more females have full-time employment; and awareness of the consequences of false allegations made against carers by children has increased.

Issues for children living in residential care

Since it was clear that there was a scarcity of foster care placements for children it was important to examine issues that arose for cross-community children when they moved to residential care. Interestingly, six out of the seven parents who expressed dissatisfaction with placements had children living in residential homes. Parents were concerned about: the inability of staff to teach their child realistic expectations of living with a family or living independently; indifferent approaches to discipline; their child's increased involvement in criminal activity since moving to residential care; their child's unhappiness living in residential care; the influence of peers in the residential home; bullying within the home; and their child's lack of a sense of belonging. One parent was particularly concerned that their child's unhappiness at a residential home had not been properly addressed:

> We were not happy at all with that. We saw him once a week supervised but that gradually increased. It was a battle to take him out. I would arrive and he wouldn't be there or they would have arranged something else for him to go to. I could take him out you see because he was in voluntary care. I kept going back until I got him out. The boys were separated and [son] went to a family. [other son] tried to commit suicide in [a residential home] and they ignored it and wanted it hush hush. It is a pure kip and should be closed down.
> **(Father of looked after child)**

Social workers also highlighted particular issues that cross-community children faced in residential care. Five social workers underlined the impact of living in homes situated in segregated areas. These social workers felt this restricted the range of social outlets for children who were looked after and sometimes placed them at risk:

> It depends on the site. There are times where I have had children here go to different places with Rangers and Celtic tops on … and they would ask if it is safe to go out on the street wearing a Celtic scarf. [Protestant child] won't go to the cityside. He goes to the Protestant shopping centre and [Catholic child] only goes to the Catholic shopping centre. I take them to play racket ball and it's the same with the leisure centres we use.
> **(Residential Social Worker)**

One social worker explained that some cross-community children developed competent ways of dealing with restricted social spaces by adapting their religious identity to suit different peer settings.

> He is switching the religious background of his peers because of where he is living. Going out for the Twelfth [of July marches] would have been alien to him a couple of years ago but he does it now to blend in and have many friends and mix but he doesn't keep friends because he's too loud but he can switch between peers. He got beat up – he was shouting slogans – twice at home, which is a hotspot, by the IRA. He changes his Celtic Football Club ring to a Protestant one when he is at the ice bowl and that has been raised with social workers but it's not an issue and it's easy for him.
> **(Residential Social Worker)**

> It is about that thing of not being sure exactly where you do fit in. Feeling estranged from one section and maybe estranged from the other section of the community as well. With [key child], for example, he very much professes to be from the Roman Catholic tradition yet he would wear Rangers tops and stuff like that so there is a sort of confusion within his own. I think he does that to maybe endear himself to the community that he is living in which would be predominantly Protestant. He finds it difficult so he professes to be from one community but yet outwardly it would make you think that he was from another. I think it is probably a lot to do with basic survival, maybe he finds it easier to survive by doing that.
> **(Residential Social Worker)**

> I know another child who was baptised a Catholic, but everything about him is Protestant and he will tell people that he is embarrassed that he was baptised Catholic that he is a Protestant. It is safer to be Protestant and easier to make friends out here when you're Protestant.
> **(Residential Social Worker)**

Likewise, children explained that being cross-community was useful because they could adapt their religious identity according to the community they were placed in to keep themselves safe:

> I could act Catholic or Protestant because Catholic and Protestant kids ask what you are.
> *(16-year-old male – residential care)*

However, social workers emphasised the detrimental impact of placing children in residential homes that were within Loyalist or Republican community areas which pressurised cross-community children to adopt the dominant religious identity:

> ... with the majority culture of the unit it changes the young people and the attitudes of the staff. I could certainly see where any child from whichever side of the community, comes into care and finds they are in the minority, might well feel pressured, and frightened and unable to express. I talked with him about it and I think he has had to change and adjust ... On one occasion someone scratched UVF on to his door. I had been off but when I came back I was appalled that it hadn't been painted over. To leave it, accept it. But I did wonder what if he scraped IRA on someone else's door would the same thing have happened? He being a yes person doesn't want a rumpus and doesn't want to get people into a row. When the rooms moved he got a chance to pick his own wallpaper and stuff but the curtains were still red, white and blue from the previous occupier who was a staunch Loyalist. It was others that noticed and he was asked after that and he said it didn't matter. But he will say sometimes that it doesn't matter when really it does in the long term ... because being in this area it is very, very difficult to have friends unless you are a Protestant.
> **(Residential Social Worker)**

> I think it is to do with geography, we are in a predominately Protestant area therefore most of the children are Protestant but we have some Catholic children ... where a home is can dictate exactly what sort of issues are going to come up in that home. I feel that very much here and you would see

> kids from Catholic backgrounds getting involved in the Twelfth marches and stuff which you wouldn't see if they were geographically in their own area.
> *(Residential Social Worker)*

> [residential home] is close to a Loyalist estate and there are Catholic girls staying there that are not getting their religious needs met and are not getting to Mass. There is one at a Protestant school in a special class and she has no contact with the Catholic religion at all. She would only get one-off Mass attendance with staff.
> *(Field Social Worker)*

Many residential social workers emphasised the impact of peer group pressure within residential homes on children's developing religious and cultural identity.

> The culture that they came from, that's not as big an impact as the culture of the unit itself that they are going to and they do become part of that culture to be acceptable ... and at the moment nobody goes [to church] – so let's assume that someone is being pressured, the culture being to stop going when they have been going, a short-term goal is to use whatever means to try and encourage that continuation. Often when it comes to peer pressure it is a no win there.
> *(Residential Social Worker)*

> The peer group influences in a group home are very strong ... I suppose the most we can do then is to tell the child that they have to be an individual, it's very hard to resist group pressure.
> *(Residential Social Worker)*

One residential social worker described a case where a Catholic girl changed her religious identity to Protestantism because she lived at a residential home beside a Loyalist estate and wanted to fit in with peers in that area. However, she explained this young person had to participate in sectarian activities to prove she could be part of their culture before she was accepted. She also described some of the challenges staff working at that residential home faced with regard to sectarianism:

> The openness does tend to be restricted, you know, they're not able to express who they are, they have very much closeted their Catholic background and maybe promoted their Protestant side to fit into the culture that is here. Our kids are active out of the community and it's very scary to deal with so much hatred and people had no tolerance whatsoever … and Catholic children and staff were being threatened. But a lot of people would flag that up at admission meetings, you know, the health and safety issues, that would be around placing a Catholic child in this environment and the Catholic staff especially. You know, they are subjected to threats and taunting from the paramilitaries and all the expletives are used … for example we had a couple of guys they were very very active in the community and getting into trouble and the local quarterhouse master you know came to the door and said 'If you can't control these kids' … And we were like 'What can we do?' Or do we take the beating for them, you know how do you deal with that? … at the height it was so bad in here that the young ones were passing on names of Catholic staff and children and cross-community children to the paramilitaries like people were being threatened and they knew their names. It was very scary. Overall religion is glazed over because it's too contentious … I don't know how to break that down, but as a social worker you would appreciate any sort of literature or programmes that enables me to maybe to choose my practice and accommodate these issues more because we do get a lot of them. And you don't need to stand out in your peer group. You want to blend in.
> ***(Residential Social Worker)***

Generally, residential social workers felt that cross-community children would experience discrimination from other children living in the home if their mixed background was known.

> … young people find out that someone is different, so [they'll] slag off their parents. If they found out that someone had come from a mixed marriage into this children's home they'd have a go …
> ***(Residential Social Worker)***

> [key child] always in pensive moments would think about the loss of experience and why was my Daddy a Catholic and why was my Mummy Protestant. So there's issues of confusion and identity but also emotional, psychological issues from the child. I guess you've more overt prejudice … being the target for name-calling and so on. Certainly I can think of another child with his Loyalist band music coming out of the windows. A couple of other teenagers were having a laugh at him in jest and he knew what they were laughing at it. You are going up to your Fenian mother and you are coming back here playing your God Save the Queen music.
> *(Residential Social Worker)*

Residential social workers felt they had to negotiate between encouraging children to express their religious and cultural identities and preventing them causing offence to other children living in the home. Social workers in residential homes close to Loyalist or Republican estates or interface areas found it difficult to maintain a neutral, anti-sectarian setting for cross-community children. They also found it hard to ensure children's safety when they entered different community areas. These difficulties were further heightened at particular times of the year when sectarian tensions were high or cultural identity was celebrated publicly for example, band parades.

> I think because of the way Northern Ireland is sort of ghettoised because of the boundaries that are there even though they're not always seen, the ratio within this unit, children-wise, would be eighty per cent Protestant and twenty per cent Catholic roughly, and because the kids are so prejudiced in their views its oppressing Catholic children – so they're going to be reluctant to say where they're from or to talk about their background. They're also less likely to be heading with any of the kids in here to that area, so it's a whole form of almost structural oppression if you like, it's very difficult for us to manage really … we take the children away from the unit which is almost an oppression because some of the kids go see the bands and that was an issue for [key child], that he was almost being made to go on the holiday when he wanted to stay here to watch the bands, I just think it's at a superficial level – to him it's almost like a

> social thing and it's fun, it's entertainment, it's something to do, you know, he doesn't have a lot of money, it doesn't cost much money to get a brick and throw it at someone, you know … it's good craic … These kids don't have the facilities that they should have in the area, there's nothing down in this estate, so again the lack of opportunities for these kids to come together.
> *(Residential Social Worker)*

> certainly the young people at times find the paramilitary side of things quite attractive for them to demonstrate that they are interested in these kind of more extremes of demonstrating their cultural background and that is a difficulty and children do get drawn to the paramilitary organisations.
> *(Field Social Worker)*

It also seemed that different residential homes had different policies regarding promotion of children's religious and cultural identity. These related to being allowed to exhibit religious or cultural symbols that may offend other children living in the home and promoting attendance at religious ceremonies.

> We are the only unit that allows expression of some identity than none, for example UVF or IRA materials ... It emerged because one child came here as the only Protestant resident … given the fact that his father was UVF background and his father died. He is isolated from the rest of the kids. It was deemed as a part of the process allowing to grieve for his father in that he be allowed to put certain things up on the wall and his father's Orange sash and a Union Jack on his wall and bits and pieces of paraphernalia. It has gone a little bit overboard I have to say but we had other children coming in who were politically active and they see him wearing a Rangers top and decided 'Well I am going to have a tricolour flag over my bedroom door' and it is an issue that is not totally resolved yet amongst the staff or amongst the children as a group. At present we are allowing it to exist because it's some expression perhaps better than no expression at all … It is certainly difficult but we try very very

> hard to maintain neutrality within the unit ... And it is difficult for children from mixed religions because there is very clearly a Protestant and Catholic division here in times of the year when these things are heightened and it is difficult because they don't belong in either or they will then choose at that point to belong to one or the other. Religion is never mentioned by the children but culture is mentioned and it is much more ...
> *(Residential Social Worker)*

> The Trust's line is they're not allowed to wear Celtic and Rangers shirts but they get them for Christmas ... but the general feeling of the staff was that we would prefer to encourage a positive reflection of cultural identity.
> *(Residential Social Worker)*

Looked after children living in residential placements described their specific experiences of sectarian tensions. One child objected to not being allowed to wear a Celtic football shirt given to him by his mother although he also owned a Rangers shirt given to him by his father. Two Catholic children living in a residential home close to a Loyalist housing estate had been physically attacked by people living in that estate. Another child living in a residential home close to a Loyalist area explained why Catholic children could not live in that home:

> One time there was a Catholic here before when I came in and the paras came up and told them to get out and they had to go or they'd get shot. Everybody knows.
> *(14-year-old male – residential care)*

Several children living in residential care mentioned that they had been involved in sectarian riots usually because it was good fun:

> It's good when I'm brought into it. I'm a fighting man and it's good craic.
> *Interviewer: Which side would you be against in the fighting?*
> I wouldn't like the Catholics.
> *Interviewer: Even though your mum's Catholic?*
> Not my family. I like those that are my family but not the Catholics that are fighting.
> *(12-year-old male – residential care)*

> I have laughed about it because I don't really care.
> Sometimes I get involved but it's not really serious.
> *(14-year-old male – residential care)*

Placements and decisions about children's education

Almost one third of looked after children had changed schools, usually for practical reasons to suit placements they had moved to. More than half of these children felt they had lost friends during these moves, however all of them made new friends at their next school. Parents of children who began school after they had become looked after generally seemed to have had little involvement in making decisions about their child's education. When foster carers decided about the child's school they usually selected the school that matched the child's religious upbringing when possible, or the birth parents' wishes or the school their own children attended. In one case, foster carers disagreed with the child's birth parent about attending a controlled school because they felt the child was being isolated from Catholic peers in the local area. In the end, her parents allowed this carer to change the child's school. Foster carers had also experienced difficulties with clergy regarding baptism and religious teaching for children who were not attending Catholic maintained schools:

> The priest nearly insisted that we take him out of the integrated school and put him in the Catholic school. I explained to him that that was the school that suited his Mum and that Mum herself was not a practising Catholic … but the response I got from the Catholic church was very negative. Many of the children in [child's] class are Catholic and the position there is that the priest won't go into the school. The priest will not even do Holy Communion for them. They want them to go to Catholic maintained schools. We had a similar problem with another child and Mum wanted the child baptised. I spoke to the Presbyterian Church. It was the pastor that was asked and he was very ignorant and wouldn't baptise the child.
> *(Foster carer)*

Generally, Catholic children attending Protestant schools found it difficult to access religious teaching on specific religious celebrations from priests.

> I went to see the schools with the foster mother and I chose a Protestant school because I felt that's where he would get the best education. I had to go to the other priest for the communion and his confirmation. The priest down there won't take any part in things like that or go to a Protestant school. I thought that was disgusting. I don't think they should mind what school a child goes to – you should be allowed to go to the school that is better … yet that priest was saying he wouldn't do any instructions for his confirmation now.
> *(Mother of looked after child)*

On the other hand, one Protestant child who went to a Catholic maintained school felt under pressure to participate in Catholic ceremonies and keep her religious identity a secret:

> I didn't tell everybody, just friends … I was mad then and I rebelled against it and wrecked the place. It was run by nuns and they insisted on me making my communion to get into the school but I refused. I wasn't gonna put on a white dress at that age to do that. The rest of the ones there had done that when they were younger.
> *(21-year-old female – leaving care)*

Parental contact issues

When possible, family contact was seen as an important aspect of promoting cross-community children's religious and cultural identity. Foster carers explained parental contact was positive for children because it maintained a sense of belonging to their birth family.

> It's great because they don't feel left out in the cold. Family contact is very good so they don't feel cut off at all.
> *(Carer)*

> To know that she is well and that her Mummy still loves her. I know that was the most important to her.
> *(Carer)*

However, for several cross-community children actually visiting their parents in other community areas was risky. These children often felt threatened entering other community areas on parental contact visits:

> … you are walking through the street and it's red, white and blue. It is sort of you feel strange walking through an area that you know that you shouldn't be in. You shouldn't be there because … you don't have family there. You would be spotted because you are not from that area.
> *(17-year-old male – foster care)*

Reflecting this child's perspective, his carer was also particularly concerned about his safety when he visited his mother:

> Ones followed him in the estate so I will never let that happen again. My husband would always drop him over and pick him up now … they just were waiting to get the bus but it is not happening again.
> *(Carer)*

Although parental contact could be positive, there were particular difficulties when parents had separated and formed new relationships. In five cases the looked after child's mother had formed a new relationship and in one case the child's father had. Overall, half of these parents formed another cross-community relationship and half had partnered with someone from the same original religious background as themselves. In three of these cases, step-relationships were problematic and difficulties were directly related to the religious background of the child's stepfather. In one case, a Protestant mother had re-married someone from the same religious background who had strong Loyalist beliefs, however her children had been placed with Catholic foster families who had strong Republican beliefs:

> *Interviewer: And does she have a new partner now?*
> Yes. I fall out with him more times.
> *Interviewer: What do you fall out about?*
> About different things like being a Catholic and carrying a flag in the [Republican] band. We'd just be teasing each other but with a thick temper he responds and he's thick and we both shout … He has a problem with me going on the Catholic parades. He wouldn't like me going to the Bloody Sunday parade but I don't mention it.
> *(16-year-old male – foster care)*

These children's carers were also aware of the impact of different cultural and political beliefs on their relationship with their mother and stepfather:

> He has a Celtic tee shirt and he would wear it down to see his mum just to annoy her husband and ones have said to her husband you know 'What are you doing with that Fenian here with that shirt on?' We just tell him to ignore it but he has a quick temper. He knows what it means to wear it and wears it to see the reaction there. Another thing was he wanted to be in a band and he was supposed to carry the flag at the front so I told him 'Don't tell your mum and [her husband]'. I think he hasn't but he might tell them.
> *(Carer)*

> The only negative thing would be when they visit their mother it upsets them especially around the twelfth of July because her husband would slag off the children. They're very much to the other side. It's a pity because it should never be mentioned.
> *(Carer)*

In another case, a Catholic mother formed another cross-community relationship and her Catholic child, who affiliated with Republicanism, found it difficult to accept his stepfather's political beliefs:

> I don't like him.
> *Interviewer: Why is that?*
> He's bitter. He even threatens me with the paramilitaries if I don't behave myself. He said that he'd get the boys on me but he doesn't know what he's talking about.
> *(16-year-old male – residential care)*

Sibling contact issues

Of the 34 children involved in this study, 28 had full siblings. Of these, 17 had regular contact with their siblings, four had contact several times per year, five had yearly contact and two had no contact. (Only eight of the 17 who had regular contact with their siblings were part of the sibling sets interviewed.) Only three children lived in the same placement as some of their siblings and four children lived in the same placement as all of their siblings. All of these children were in foster care. Other children reported mixed feelings towards sibling contact. Some children were happy with contact even though it was not regular. Others were unhappy that contact was irregular and felt they did not have enough contact with their siblings. Children who had been looked after on a long-term basis and had infrequent contact with their siblings over the years explained that they found contact difficult because they no longer knew their siblings or had nothing in common with them.

> I haven't seen my sister for a couple of years maybe three years. I was visiting her but she didn't know who I was.
> *(12-year-old male – foster care)*

None of the parents of looked after children were unhappy about sibling contact between their children. Likewise, foster carers were generally pleased with sibling contact arrangements and only raised two issues. Firstly, they felt it was often difficult to organise sibling contact due to practical constraints. Secondly, they explained that sometimes sibling relationships were strained because they had little in common or due to challenging behaviour from a sibling.

Social workers' views on parental and sibling contact

Some social workers also raised issues for parental and sibling contact, such as the practical constraints of organising contact:

> It's more the time that contact requires, transport, supervision and keeping parents committed to it.
> *(Field Social Worker)*

Three social workers explained they did not experience any problems with parental contact because the child only had contact with one parent so there was less opportunity for parental disagreements or conflicting opinions on the upbringing of the child. However, one social worker felt that sometimes only having one parent actively involved in contact made things more difficult because usually in those cases parents have separated and there were tensions between each parent's family.

When children were separated from their siblings they were more likely to adopt the religious identity of their foster carer. This meant that siblings were raised with different religious identities. Two social workers suggested this had not caused any significant difficulties, although in one of these cases the child is the only Catholic in a Loyalist family:

> I would have had that child who is Catholic and his siblings are Protestant. His mum was the Protestant and dad was the Catholic and there was a sectarian murder of the dad. Mum would have been a Loyalist but her family live in a Catholic area. He knows his dad's extended family and visits them and goes to Mass with them.
> ***Interviewer: How does that child make sense of all of that?***
> … he knows that his mother is not the same religion to himself and his daddy, he was brought up in the Catholic faith and made first communion and his first confirmation, and he knows. I don't think it ever entered his wee head though on contact and it was just his mum is still an important person regardless of religion … I mean his confirmation he had his mum there that day.
> **(Field Social Worker)**

Other social workers were unsure how siblings dealt with having different religious upbringing but imagined there would be difficulties for such sibling groups especially at times when there are sectarian tensions, when children became involved in different cultural activities or when children are celebrating different religious ceremonies:

> I suppose that can be maybe more difficult with siblings because children or young people at times don't think about things that they say and would offend the other person … and when you're having contact with their siblings that could be very difficult especially when the marching season starts that can be really difficult. I suppose it would be difficult too in terms of religion to be able to talk about it because perhaps they might be more aware and warned by foster parents don't say anything about that or do that. They are meaning well because they don't want to offend but then issues are never brought up and they're not learning any more about their siblings or – I suppose if the sibling was making something like confirmation too then that would raise an issue as well if siblings come along to that ceremony.
> **(Field Social Worker)**

Five social workers used case examples to explain how particular problems with contact arise when parents and children disagreed on the religious upbringing of the child:

> He has really distanced himself from his mum and is choosing not to have her there ... and we don't have much contact with her. He avoids mum and that situation and flaunts Protestant memorabilia in front of his Catholic mum or granny. She can't understand because she's Catholic.
> *(Field Social Worker)*

> I can see it is awful for the child and the young person involved because they are pulled two ways and ... it is the adults in many ways who ... continue to put them through the emotional trauma of being at loggerheads, pulling in two different directions ... I've worked with young people where the parents are at loggerheads and they run in two directions, and the child is caught right in the middle of that.
> *(Residential Social Worker)*

Eight social workers claimed that contact also became difficult when children, parents or external family members held strong religious and/or political beliefs or when the area the child or family lived in was particularly Loyalist or Republican. This sometimes caused conflict between family members and the child:

> In these areas families are usually already so split so like [key child] has no contact with his dad and there is no relationship there. It's very difficult when they are aligned to one community and his dad is aware of that – that the family is aligned with the opposite community and he wishes to have very minimal contact. [key child] wants to see his dad and sought him out but contact broke down because of the two communities and [key child] being placed at risk, entering where his dad lived would be very risky for him but that's hard to explain to him and he gets confused with that ... Because their families are so staunch there was an automatic relationship cut off because of family pressure. When his mum and dad's relationship came to the families' attention with the pregnancy it was stopped.
> *(Field Social Worker)*

> ... that can be very difficult because it can be threats of violence or aggression or hostility around in the background. We have one child whose mum is in a relationship with someone whose very Loyalist so a Catholic girl went to live with mum in a Loyalist area and there was internal conflict and turmoil and it was a big issue. While she was there her safety was guaranteed. Now she has left and she was told she couldn't come back.
> *(Field Social Worker)*

However, some social workers' comments suggested they were unaware of some of the issues cross-community children had faced. For example, one Catholic child felt intimidated and unsafe when he visited his mother in a Loyalist area, however, his social worker believed he had no difficulty and this was the most appropriate venue for contact visits:

> Usually at the mum's house because there are no venues for Protestant families to go to the cityside. He has lived in a Catholic area beforehand and then a mixed area but he goes there [to his mother's house] off his own bat. It doesn't bother him.
> *(Field Social Worker)*

This demonstrates the lack of communication between children and social workers about issues relating to religious and cultural identity or sectarian danger. Only three social workers acknowledged that it was important to consider risk for cross-community children when arranging family contact visits:

> The location of contact can be very hard. For example the family centre is in a Loyalist area so for Catholic kids it's not child-friendly because they can't even walk their kids outside … There can also be difficulties when parents are voicing uncertainty or negativity about carers or the area.
> *(Field Social Worker)*

> It is the confusion about what is the right thing to do and say and what can I do to avoid trouble and they are not quite sure what is the safe line here. So it does add to the difficulty.
> *(Field Social Worker)*

Principal social workers outlined the policy on parental and sibling contact that governed social work practice. They discussed the duties within the Children

(NI) Order 1995, the use of the 'looked after' review process for defining the frequency and nature of family contact and the need to consider reviewing placements for sibling groups at the same time.

> Throughout the Looked After Children (LAC) forms and the care plans, etc., there is a very specific area to address contact arrangements ... I suppose it's back to limited placements and because we don't have foster placements we end up splitting groups into different foster homes. I think what tends to happen is at reviews if there's a sibling albeit with a separate placement they should look at them at the same time so they shouldn't really lose sight of the total picture. But ... we should be saying that children in both these families should be brought up as one religion and not necessarily find that situation in the long term with one child from one background and one from the other because I don't doubt it would create difficulties for them in later years, certainly impacting on their relationship in the longer term. I'm not aware of the extent to which we're addressing those at our reviews.
> *(Principal Social Worker)*

External family contact issues

Almost half of the looked after children still had contact with external family members, however, 14 out of the 34 children interviewed had lost such contact. Some children would have liked an opportunity to meet more of their external family members, however others did not mind not having contact with external family:

> No they were never involved with us.
> *(21-year-old female – leaving care)*

> I used to always see my granny. I haven't for a long time now. It doesn't bother me.
> *(17-year-old male – foster care)*

Some children had very positive and frequent contact with external family members. Indeed, one child was fostered by his aunt; and two children were fostered by their grandparents. Excluding external family who were carers, five children felt they had close contact with aunts and eight children felt they had close relationships with their grandparents. However, none of these children had close contact with external family on both sides of their family. The majority of children only had contact with their paternal external family. Indeed, one parent of looked after children expressed dissatisfaction with contact their children had with external family members because she felt social workers only prioritised contact with one side of the family:

> She used to see my mum and dad but it stopped. I asked about her going to them again and they said they'd ring but … they haven't rang … she could visit cos my parents would love to have the child down but they never got back. She sees a lot of her dad's family and I'm not happy about that.
> ***(Mother of looked after child)***

Foster carers were also generally positive about contact children had with external family members. However, reflecting findings from children, several carers noted that children usually only had contact with external family on one side of their family background:

> They have a grandad and he's very nice. She would see him once a month because her father would bring them up to him – it's his own father. He never forgets them and always asks about them. There would be aunties and uncles in the father's as well when she goes down there … There wouldn't be much contact with wider family on her [mother's] side and on the dad's side it would be very positive especially with their grandfather. He makes a lot to do with them and brings them to see their granny's grave and all.
> ***(Carer)***

> All the father's ones just … He has no contact with his other side [mother's] and they've never asked to see any of the children … they never called to see them.
> ***(Carer)***

Seven social workers also recognised that cross-community children tended to only maintain contact with one side of their external family relatives. This was usually the family that matched the chosen religious identity for the child or the most dominant family side.

> Children would have more contact with those who match the identity of their decided religion and lose contact with the others because of safety issues and fear.
> *(Residential Social Worker)*

> In his case there's more issues with the external family because it is divided and he has chosen Protestant so her side don't really bother. It really depends on him to visit his Catholic family and siblings because they don't come to him apart from the oldest.
> *(Field Social Worker)*

> She's accepted as a part of her father's family … she's her father's daughter and they glaze over the Catholic bit. She doesn't go to see her mum's side of the family pretty much, since she's come in here the contact has stopped.
> *(Residential Social Worker)*

Again, geographical and practical constraints impacted on facilitation of contact with external family. Difficulties also arose when children had to enter predominantly Loyalist or Republican areas to visit external family or when external family members imposed strong religious or political beliefs on children:

> If external family have strong beliefs they might put the children under pressure to be one way or another and we need to ensure that the children feel free.
> *(Field Social Worker)*

Principal social workers outlined the policy guidance available on external family contact. Such contact depended on the significance of the role of external family in the child's life and resource constraints.

> The Children Order would encourage us to maintain contact with grandparents. I mean parental responsibility can be split so that concept would make us focus in on the wider extended family but again it's going back to the contact being beneficial to the child … that's quite a commitment for us, the social worker could spend the whole week just facilitating contact so … we've got a contact service at the moment but we'd certainly be looking for resources to develop that.
> *(Principal Social Worker)*

Summary

The majority of social workers confirmed that case files were often inaccurate or incomplete. They suggested this was because information was not available or they did not prioritise or have time to complete records. In addition, more than half of the social workers suggested religious identity was often assumed based on the schools children attended, their name or the area they lived in. Inaccurate records of children's religious identity may be related to the fact that most social workers found it difficult to consult parents and children about their religious identity. This was particularly challenging when families held strong political or sectarian beliefs, families made assumptions about social workers' religious identity or parents could not decide about their religious identity. Consulting children was also difficult when children expressed sectarian attitudes or associated decisions about religious identity with their feelings for their parents. Social workers felt uncomfortable asking questions about religion and culture because they viewed it as a sensitive and private issue in the context of a divided society.

Social workers emphasised that resource constraints and limited numbers of carers restricted placement choices for cross-community children who were looked after. Therefore, social workers prioritised other needs of these children and gave their religious and cultural needs a low priority. When children became looked after, parents felt they had little input into decisions about their education. As most schools were segregated this was a key decision impacting on children's religious and cultural identity. Being placed in segregated areas or attending segregated schools restricted opportunities for children to develop mixed friendships across communities. Children living in residential care also experienced additional challenges as they were more likely to feel under pressure to choose the dominant religion of others living in the home or in that community area. The interviews point to a worrying level of sectarianism within residential care, with staff unsure of how to handle this. Social workers emphasised that cross-community children learnt effective ways of disguising or adapting their religious identity when they entered segregated spaces.

Parents were dissatisfied when they were not involved in important decisions about their children's religious upbringing. Siblings who were also looked after were often separated into various placements and often adopted different religious identities to match the religious background of their carers. Social workers highlighted how this created difficulties when sectarian tensions were high or siblings were participating in religious and cultural activities. Children felt that contact with their siblings was important, however if they had infrequent contact with their siblings for long periods of time they felt that subsequent contact was strained. Contact with external family members was positive, children usually only maintained contact with one side of their family. This was usually the most dominant family side or the side that matched the religious identity of the child. Additionally, several children had negative relationships with their step-parents because of their religious and/or political beliefs.

Overall, three major factors influenced family contact. Firstly, there were practical difficulties of arranging contact with family who were living long distances away. This was particularly relevant to cross-community children whose parents had separated and were living in opposite sides of the community. Secondly, disagreements between children and parents about the child's religious identity impacted on family contact, especially since these disagreements were often related to the children's feelings about their parents. Finally, when family members had strong political beliefs or lived in areas that were predominantly Loyalist or Republican contact became difficult and unsafe.

7. Promoting the religious and cultural identity of looked after children

This chapter discusses approaches to promoting religious and cultural identity of looked after children as outlined in the Children (NI) Order (1995). This will include identification of the main factors influencing the religious and cultural upbringing of cross-community children who become looked after, such as the religious and community background of foster carers. This chapter also discusses the training needs of foster carers and social workers in relation to promoting positive identities for cross-community children and addressing sectarianism.

Religious upbringing of looked after children

Of the looked after children involved in the study, 17 had adopted their father's religious identity. In nine of these cases their father was Protestant and in eight cases Catholic. Sixteen of the children had the same religious identity as their mother. In half of these cases, their mother was Catholic and in the other half Protestant. In 13 cases one parent acted as the main carer for their child before they became looked after. This was usually because parents had separated or one parent had never had contact with the child. In 12 of these cases the child's mother was the main carer. Only one out of these 13 children did not follow the same religious identity as the parent acting as their main carer. However, decisions about looked after children's religious and cultural identity were not based solely on parental background. Other factors such as location of placement and religious backgrounds of carers also impacted on these decisions.

Some parents of looked after children were concerned that their children could be confused about their identity or feel they have to hide one part of their identity. This was mainly because of other influences, such as only having contact with one side of their family or living in an area where people were predominantly from one religious background.

> Well one day in the car she said to me 'Am I a Protestant or a Catholic?', you see she sees a lot of her dad's family and I don't really want her to be down there because I don't know what they're saying to them. The grandad told her sister to say 'F**k the pope'. They're drumming things into her that I don't like so I don't like her going down there … She went to Catholic Mass and was christened Catholic and was at a Catholic school but now goes to [residential home in Loyalist area]. Her sister was Catholic and when she went to [residential home in Loyalist area] she turned Protestant because she was more at her father's place and was going with a wee fella from that area.
> *(Mother of looked after child)*

Half of the parents of looked after children were satisfied with the religious upbringing of their children. This was largely because their wishes had been taken into consideration and adhered to, especially in relation to attendance at church services:

> It didn't have to turn into an argument or anything, I just insisted that he was to Mass every week and they've done it … Before he was put into long-term care it was discussed, you know, was I happy for him to stay along with a Protestant family or did I want to have a Catholic, but he was happy where he was, so … I'd rather him have his happiness, were it that he had a Catholic family where maybe he might not have been so happy. I mean I could have been difficult and said 'No, I want him in a Catholic family. I don't want him to stay with a Protestant family' but I mean he's happy so why upset the child further.
> *(Mother of looked after child)*

The other half of parents of looked after children were unhappy about their child's religious upbringing when they became looked after. This was for several reasons: because they had not been involved in decisions about their children's religious upbringing; the placements children moved to dictated their religious identity; their child had developed more sectarian attitudes; their child was not attending religious ceremonies as they did at home or carers did not actively promote their religious and cultural identity.

> He has now become very Catholic, very very because of where he was staying and the schools he was at. He's very down on Protestants although he has Protestant friends … I mean it's only in the last four years he stopped calling [protestant stepfather] Dad, you know. 'You're not my f**king dad, you're an Orangeman and a hun'… When he was in [residential home in Republican area] he then became strictly Catholic – he didn't want anyone to know he was mixed … At the minute he's in [residential home in Loyalist area] and just doesn't tell anybody anything where he's at, because he knows the difference. That's very Protestant and he knows the dangers there.
> **(Mother of looked after child)**

> I've yet to hear of him going to church on Sunday … but he should because if he was at home he would be going.
> **(Mother of looked after child)**

> I wanted them all to be Catholics but the other two changed to Protestant and they're talking to her about changing religion and I don't want them to but they'll do it anyway.
> **(Mother of looked after child)**

> They would come to the Twelfth [of July Parade] with us but [daughter] causes a big row and refuses to go … the foster parents won't let her be open to the Protestant faith. She has to be Catholic and they've that drummed into her to have nothing to do with Protestants.
> **(Mother of looked after child)**

As the quotations below illustrate, findings from interviews with children accorded with parental concerns:

> Children believe different things and they wouldn't know what to believe in. One parent was telling one thing and the other was telling something else. It would be difficult cos it's your mum and dad … not for me because I knew I wanted to be like my foster family – be Catholic.
> **(14-year-old female – foster care)**

> A couple of people shout things and I got beaten up once ... when I was in [residential home in Loyalist area].
> *(Ten-year-old male – foster care)*

Looked after children's experience of religious and cultural upbringing

Looked after children had mixed experiences of religious upbringing that often changed when they moved between placements. One child living in a residential home explained that he only had to attend Mass when he was at home with his family and not at the residential home. In contrast, another child explained that when she lived in a different residential home she was forced to attend Mass but now that she had returned home she had more choice and did not go as regularly:

> I'm Catholic. In the home they used to make you go and I hated that cos if you didn't go you got grounded and you didn't get pocket money. Here you have a choice and we only go on special occasions or if someone is sick.
> *(14-year-old female – home on Care Order)*

When one parent had decided about children's religious upbringing this had implications for supporting their identity when they became looked after – especially if children only had contact with the parent who had not decided and was not from that religious background.

> I went with whatever he [husband] wanted. When we were together I didn't mind. But now I do mind. I wish I had brought him up in Catholic religion ... because I'm a Catholic and I'd like him to be, it's too late now – like if he came to ask me about Protestant religion I wouldn't have a notion ... you see we never really talked much about it, he [husband] said he wanted him to be brought up in his religion, fair enough, no problem. But then I thought we'd be together forever.
> *(Mother of looked after child)*

Thirteen children commented on changing their religious identity. One young person had stopped practising Catholicism when she moved to a residential home:

> I used to be Catholic religion but not anymore. Here you can't. You can't listen to Catholic music or anything since I came here and the staff here are very mixed.
> ***(16-year-old female – residential care)***

Several looked after children had practised both Catholicism and Protestantism depending on their placement. The child quoted below was reared as a Catholic when he lived with a Catholic carer, then as Protestant when he later moved to kinship foster care. Although he seemed unaware that he had been raised with different religious identities, his experience in a Catholic church illustrated cultural differences:

> I went to Chapel with [previous foster carer]. But they chucked me out because I was making noises and one day I was talking about King Billy and all and we go in band parades and the priest sent me away … I don't mind because I was only young and it was boring going to Chapel. You had to sit and say your prayers and all and you had to sing.
> ***(Ten-year-old male – foster care)***

Two children discussed feeling under pressure to follow the religious identity their parent preferred:

> My Mum tried to bring me up a Catholic. I didn't like that. She was trying to make me do something I didn't want.
> ***(17-year-old male – residential care)***

> ***Interviewer: Did you ever change your religion?***
> No. My mummy told me not to because she wants me to be a Catholic.
> ***(11-year-old female – residential care)***

Even children who had contact with family from both religious backgrounds felt they had to choose one religious identity to fit into Northern Irish society:

> Mum is Protestant and Dad is Catholic. I was baptised Catholic but I grew up with Mum. Then when I was ten I moved to Dad's for a while and then three foster carers and they were all Catholic and then back to Mum for just a week. I went to Protestant primary school cos I lived with Mum. Then I went to a Catholic secondary school. I even went there when I lived with my mum … For ages I used to

> say I was an atheist but then I picked Protestant ... I was more comfortable being a Protestant ... I can't be nothing because then people think you're hiding something or there's something.
> *(21-year-old female – leaving care)*

However, some of the children who had been raised with one religious identity suggested they would prefer an identity that embraced both of their birth parents' religious backgrounds:

> My mummy had to decide whether to be a Catholic or a Protestant. It's just it depends on Mummy or Daddy. Let them argue.
> *Interviewer: Are you happy that your mummy insisted that you were Catholic?*
> Sort of. I think I'm fully Catholic but I want to be half Protestant and half Catholic because that would be half and half on Mummy's side and Daddy's side, but I don't know.
> *(11-year-old female – residential care)*

Another child who had lived in both Catholic and Protestant placements suggested this should be advocated for looked after children as it broadens their knowledge about both communities and teaches them to be less sectarian:

> When you go into foster care they ask you do you want to be Catholic or Protestant and match you with those carers but I think they should send Catholic children to Protestant homes and Protestant children to Catholic homes cos I remember one boy that happened to said he couldn't believe how nice they were. And I have got that from being at a Catholic school and because my family's all mixed I'm less bigoted and religion is not difficult for me.
> *(21-year-old female – leaving care)*

The role of foster carers in children's developing identity

Surprisingly, four carers who had looked after cross-community children on a long-term basis only discovered their cross-community background when they were approached to participate in this research. Another carer found out the child in their care was cross-community a long time after their admission to care when the child's birth parent re-married. In addition, although the majority of carers discovered the child's cross-community background when the child first arrived, they still usually viewed these children as having one religious identity. This reflects the fact that most social workers believed children should follow one religious faith.

When decisions about a child's religious upbringing were made after they had become looked after, their carers often chose to raise the child in their own religious faith and this only sometimes concurred with the specified wishes of the child.

> When it came to him being four he still wasn't christened and I thought he should have something you know so he was christened when he was five into the Church of Ireland … we suggested it and it was our own faith and his father is Protestant … the parents signed the form anyhow for it to happen.
> ***(Carer)***

> They weren't baptised or christened either so I didn't know. She was eight years old before she was baptised – just in time for her Holy Communion. She wanted to be like us and the social worker finally got round mum when she was in primary three. She expressed that wish to the social worker. One social worker wanted her brother to go to church but he didn't want to go – he wanted to be Catholic and I even think he went to Catholic families after us too.
> ***(Carer)***

In one case, where a child had changed his religious identity to match placement changes, carers assumed he did not realise any differences:

> He was going to Mass with his carer and he came to us when he was just turning four years old and we got him dedicated to the Pentecostal church every week and Sunday school. He was even in the Orange Order.
> ***(Carer)***

Indeed, two carers believed that the children in their care did not know they were from a cross-community background:

> He doesn't have a clue. He doesn't know he's from a cross-community background.
> *(Carer)*

Another carer felt that, although the child in their care knew he was from a cross-community background, things were not different for him because others in the local community were unaware of his background. Five carers felt the child in their care only had positive experiences of being cross-community. They suggested that when children accessed integrated schools and lived in neutral areas they could be effectively supported to have a positive experience of being cross-community.

> Certainly there is no negative ones that I've been aware of, if anything it is more positive in the fact she has no hang-ups about it from that point of view. She likes anybody. She is a very friendly girl. She does not care what you are because we don't care what you are.
> *(Carer)*

Negative experiences that carers felt cross-community children experienced were in relation to taunting from peers and not understanding why they were raised in a different faith from their foster family.

> He would say 'Mummy doesn't go to my church' and he used to go to Sunday school with my church but his mother said no. I think that's bad. The churches are very similar and he should see the other side. He was annoyed about it as well. He knows a lot of ones out of my church because they all live behind us here.
> *(Carer)*

> They went to the local Catholic schools. There would be some problems with teasing. They would say things like 'Your mother's only a...' Children knew. Children threw comments about them.
> *(Carer)*

Given these mixed experiences, it was important to explore how foster carers helped children to develop a positive religious and cultural identity. They felt they did this by ensuring children attended appropriate church services and schools and supporting them to participate in religious events and activities, such as Holy Communion. When the child had a different religious identity from the carer's family, other arrangements were made to facilitate the child's attendance at religious ceremonies.

> By our example, teaching in the home and they get that at school too, going to Mass and supporting them by answering questions they have. It's important to know who you are and where you are.
> *(Carer)*

Interestingly, two carers felt that they avoided discussing religious or political divisions in Northern Ireland with children in their care:

> We try to keep Protestants and Catholics away from all children but we tell them what they are. It's maybe a bad thing in a way but for me it's too negative I don't see anything positive in this so it's maybe more to do with 'me. I just, if anything, try to protect them from the negative things. If that means keeping them away from the church as such then so be it. She knows there is two different religions but she hasn't been old enough to get into depth in it yet.
> *Interviewer: Would you talk to her about what her religion is?*
> No. I don't even discuss religion. It has never been an issue with us.
> *(Carer)*

The majority of foster carers felt adequately skilled to meet the religious and cultural needs of the cross-community children in their care. This was usually because carers raised looked after children in the same way as they did their own children or they had received assistance from others, such as teachers or priests. Interestingly, none of these carers mentioned that social workers provided any particular support or advice. Other carers who did not feel adequately skilled anticipated further issues may emerge for these children as they grow older and felt they did not have enough knowledge about both religious and cultural backgrounds.

Only one carer felt that promoting a child's religious or cultural identity was a high priority for social services. Indeed, five out of the 15 carers stated that promoting a child's religious or cultural identity was never mentioned by their social worker. Surprisingly, all of these carers were happy with this approach:

> He [social worker] never mentions religion. [foster child]
> did but the social worker didn't. His other carer was Catholic
> and his dad used to go to the King Billy marches … Social
> workers didn't get involved. They couldn't have give much
> advice.
> *(Carer)*

> *Interviewer: How do you feel about their not making it a priority?*
> It wouldn't worry me. I don't know. To be honest with you
> I have never really thought about it before now.
> *(Carer)*

Most carers were pleased this was not a high priority with social services because they had adhered to the wishes of the parent or were satisfied that the children's religious needs were met at school. Carers were pleased that social services left it up to the discretion of carers to raise such matters at reviews if they became a problem.

> They tend to leave it for the foster carer. I think it's fine
> especially if the children are long-term with you. You're the
> one bringing them up and you bring them up as you would
> your own.
> *(Carer)*

However, three carers were unhappy that identity needs were not addressed by their social worker and that carers had to seek answers from social services rather than social workers actively offering information, advice or support.

> We were very aware that he was never baptised and we kept
> on at the social worker to get that sorted.
> *(Carer)*

These carers felt strongly that social workers should make greater efforts to meet the needs of children in their care. Carers wanted social workers to take the views of the child into consideration, especially when they disagreed with their parents, and focus more on the social and identity needs of children.

> I feel social workers with a foster child should focus more on
> that child … 'Are they getting bullied? Are they confident? Do
> they look down on themselves or do they blame themselves
> for that?' Are there any problems at all even with the foster
> carers, especially ones that have children of their own. That is

> a big issue … It would be nice if social workers took that child somewhere out of the foster home so he can openly speak without maybe being scared. They might be scared to say and they could be threatened at school or in a foster home or the carer's own children could be jealous .
> *(Carer)*

> I think they should listen to the child more and respect their wishes.
> *(Carer)*

Kinship foster carers felt they had different experiences to other carers because they were family members. For this reason, some of these carers felt the procedures and support for carers were inappropriate to meet their needs.

> The social worker knows I take him to church and Sunday school and they were happy enough with that. We are family so he was the same religion so I was happy about that … I think when it's family fostering it's different. Reviews and forms are not always suited to the informality of a family placement. Even support groups wouldn't be suited when it's family.
> *(Carer)*

Field social workers commented on how they would encourage foster carers to help cross-community children in their care develop a strong, positive religious and cultural identity. These social workers expected carers to adhere to agreements set out in the child's care plan, such as bringing the child to religious and cultural activities and informing them about their cross-community background.

> We encourage them to take or facilitate the child going to church or Mass and that is at least weekly with prayers and stories as well.
> *(Female Field Social Worker)*

> To give positive messages to children, verbally and non-verbally about their background. To discuss differences with the children and say that it's okay for children's parents to have differences. To be very forthcoming about religion. I mean that the child knows where they came from, knows

all about it from an early stage so that they grow up with
that. And from an early stage hopefully they've got a good
feeling of self worth so that they're able to tackle their
external issues, I'm talking here about the teasing you know
within schools, so if they have a strong belief in themselves
then they're able to deal with that.
(Field Social Worker)

However, social workers felt that some carers were better than others at promoting a child's sense of religious and cultural identity. In addition, some social workers were unsure how well they ensured carers were doing that:

Some foster carers I hazard to say are excellent and others I
have to say are nowhere near that ... It depends on their own
attitudes and views and you tease it out with them and see if
they are prepared to take this on. That is part and parcel of
their placement agreement.
(Field Social Worker)

There always seems to be more important issues to discuss
about reasons why they are in care. Those would take
preference over religion and I think again that would be
somewhere where the religion would be forgotten about.
(Field Social Worker)

Identity as a social services priority

As with carers, Figure 7.1 shows that overall only five social workers felt that promoting a looked after child's sense of religious and cultural identity was a high priority.

It would be a high priority because it's a requirement. It's a
have to do not a might do. It's vital or the child's emotional
make-up can collapse. Their history is important because
you need to know who you are to be happy with where you
are now.
(Field Social Worker)

However, even two of these social workers were concerned about the reluctance of social workers to address anti-oppressive issues both in training and practice:

Identity is important. A young person needs to know who they are, where they have come from in order to move on ... Feeling comfortable with themselves, boost their self-esteem. Makes them feel worthwhile. But I suppose in many ways what is happening now is just the filter down of the fact that we can really stick our heads in the sand, try and avoid it because it is an experience that we don't want.
(Residential Social Worker)

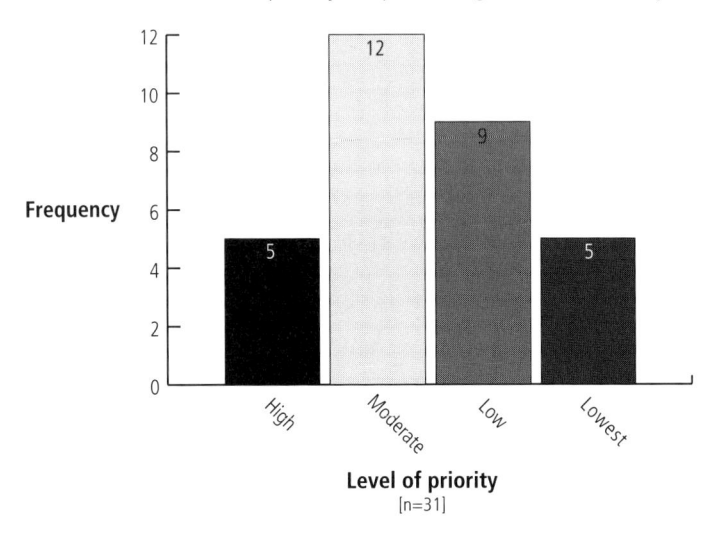

Northern Ireland social work education really needs to be looked at. I think it is looked at with social work education in England, Scotland and Wales on the race issue very very thoroughly with regard to policies and practices for social work ... they are certainly not doing the same in Northern Ireland with the difference in Protestant and Catholic.
I think that traditionally social workers come from left wing liberal and it is very hard for social workers to turn round and say 'Oh my God do you think we might not be anti-oppressive'. It is very hard to say 'Do you think we should offer an unbiased educational service?'
(Residential Social Worker)

Figure 7.1 Level of social services priority for promoting children's identity

Level of priority	Frequency
High	5
Moderate	12
Low	9
Lowest	5

[n=31]

A total of 12 social workers suggested it was a moderate priority, nine a low priority and five social workers claimed it would be the lowest of all. These social workers explained this was because of time and resource constraints and the need to address more critical issues for looked after children.

> It's one of the last on the list. I would say it's the one that doesn't change and school and education, sexualised behaviour are the priority of things I would have more in-depth conversations about. You prioritise your time. I mean if you can get the basics covered you're doing well, and it's not very often that your kids will be that well organised that you think we're going to focus on their cultural needs here … people would talk about it in a very casual way, but it's not set – maybe in life story work and ideally it should be, but realistically we have no resources and field social workers are too busy, you know you're lucky if they can come and see the child on the monthly visits … it's not that social workers don't want to address the issues, they'd probably find it really interesting, but realistically it's not possible.
> ***(Residential Social Worker)***

None of the principal social workers suggested promoting a child's sense of religious and cultural identity was a high priority. However, they felt that social work staff should be encouraged to examine these issues with children more thoroughly as an essential part of meeting children's needs.

> Most of the families we work with are from working class families and there are more important issues than religion. But the biggest one would be to get the basic care sorted and permanency. Well we have twelve children from very mixed up backgrounds in a children's home and it's a struggle to survive in residential care. For example, Catholic children shouldn't be in some of our homes but they are and it's real and you can't get away from it.
> ***(Principal Social Worker)***

> In actively receiving children in care the emphasis is on the hard stuff like a safe placement and children's trauma and anxiety. Later when it is settled we have our care plans and can look at the child's identity. We reinforce that and encourage social workers to look more at the soft side and look more at finding out about religion and ensure the child doesn't lose their identity. There is a danger that softer issues stay secondary and that needs to be picked up earlier or it won't be addressed properly.
> ***(Principal Social Worker)***

Social work role in developing children's identity

Social workers suggested they promoted children's religious and cultural identity by upholding the wishes of their parents, encouraging them to participate in religious and cultural activities and educating children about different religious beliefs and staying safe in public. However, several social workers depended heavily on schools and church attendance to provide religious teaching for children.

> Religious and cultural identity is part of their educational experience and they certainly get that on a regular basis when they go to school.
> *(Residential Social Worker)*
>
> *Interviewer: Apart from attending services is there any other way you work to ensure cross-community children have a positive religious identity?*
> No. I mean the schools all cover religious education at some time.
> *(Field Social Worker)*

Residential social workers emphasised the importance of ensuring children attended religious services and educating children who expressed sectarian attitudes. However, sometimes this raised difficulties when parents and children did not have a strong sense of their identity or when children and parents had conflicting opinions. The quotations below show how these issues created additional complexities for their work with children:

> The majority of them aren't practising. Then if you put them into care then people go back into corners. In [looked after child's] case her mother wouldn't practise any sort of religion, but she would be demanding that [looked after child] is brought up in a Catholic tradition and is very vehement and if only they listened to what [looked after child] is saying in relation to that. On whether [looked after child] will ever practise at all would be very dubious. She is in [residential home in a Loyalist area] and it's much easier to be Protestant there. She is the only Catholic long-term child there because they're not supposed to be there and

she has to be always supervised there. I think cross-community children most choose Protestant or Catholic and children's views are not listened to. Parental responsibility rules and that's sad for the kids. The chances that [looked after child] will go back to her Catholic family are slim. She has more chance of building bonds with the Protestant family but mum restricts that.
(Field Social Worker)

He [key child] would perceive himself as a Protestant. The mother is giving out continually about him not going to Mass or not taking him to Mass because that is her belief and she is the Catholic in that relationship … He was saying I don't want to go ... but he actually went to keep the peace because he knew what she was like and if he didn't go then she would disown him for about three months, so it was very difficult for him.
Interviewer: And what does his mum think about his Protestant identity?
We wouldn't make that openly known to her, he wouldn't, he doesn't say to her, you know I am Protestant.
(Residential Social Worker)

I remind him when he is being abusive to Protestants because he gets into fights with Protestants and throws stones at the police and that – that he himself has a father that comes from a Protestant background so it's not that simple. To him it's just another word or action to use – it's not about religion … He may mention occasionally he has a Protestant father and some of the more articulate older residents will say 'Why are you saying that when your father is a Protestant?' They would call that 'Jatholic'.
(Residential Social Worker)

Social workers indicated they monitored how looked after children's religious and cultural needs were met at monthly visits, individual sessions with children and looked after child reviews. However, most social workers admitted that monitoring children's religious and cultural needs usually only focused on attendance at services. This was mainly because they felt children had other needs that were more important, such as safety issues.

We don't meet needs beyond attendance. I do find there is more emphasis on the importance of Mass than there is to church attendance. The Protestant children invariably don't go to church but for the Catholic children all the stops are pulled out to ensure they go to Mass … the majority of people who work here and the majority of the managers come from a Catholic background. I would say it could be said of social work in Northern Ireland … It's more than just superficially whether or not you are going to Mass or going to church. I would like to see deeper work addressing ignorance and challenging myths like youth work programmes for young Protestant/Catholic people about positive identity and integrated group work … If I go home I discuss politics with my children but that perhaps gets left behind here, not intentionally but because we are all under huge stress to do a huge number of things in a very short period of time with a high number of very damaged children. Perhaps out of all of those things keeping them safe physically and emotionally takes enough time and there is little quality time left for religious and cultural issues.
(Residential Social Worker)

It isn't really a priority and it's not really discussed – child's health, contact, education. They're the main issues. What normally would be put on the form would be the child's religious needs are being met. I think to be honest … all the time you would just assume their religious needs were being met.
(Field Social Worker)

I have … done a bit on the identity and have come away from it thinking I went through all of the questions but there wasn't room in the questions to say 'Would you like to experience interaction with people of a different culture? Would you like to get to know them?' It is basically are your needs being met? So the forms are very much set out for the professional and have general questions but there is a lack of giving the child an opportunity to say … we are talking here as well about the spiritual issues, they don't necessarily get met through going to church, they are not particularly open to that.
(Residential Social Worker)

One residential social worker also indicated that the distinction between church attendance and religious faith was often confused. This social worker felt that the needs of cross-community children were not properly addressed and described how religious issues were sometimes the source of behavioural problems between residential staff and children:

> I don't believe we are meeting them … they are way way way down the list of needs and these children have many many needs that are much more tangible sometimes than their religious needs. Reviews monitor whether or not children are attending Mass … I do resent that a little bit because there are situations when he [key child] has become violent because certain members of staff have deep religious beliefs that it is paramount he attends Mass and that for him not to attend Mass he is in danger and they need to save his soul and they are pulling him out of bed for Mass and causing a row. A colleague was physically beaten by him because the colleague raised this issue of his soul and Mass. Sometimes … Sundays are a nightmare in residential units. They're actually called 'Suicide Sundays' because most untoward incidents, tension and violence are recorded on Sunday evenings.
> **(Residential Social Worker)**

Some social workers felt that cross-community children were more likely to experience discrimination and feel confused about their identity. To counteract these pressures these social workers suggested it was important to provide positive messages about both religious and cultural backgrounds and non-biased advice on how cross-community children could deal with sectarian experiences.

> I guess in the context of Northern Ireland they would certainly need to be educated about their respective parental backgrounds. What Catholicism is, or Protestantism is, what Unionism is, what Nationalism is so that they can resolve any sense of psychological conflict possibly that they have over their background. They would certainly have a need to understand what their rights are in terms of possible discrimination that they may possibly experience. That may occur simply in the street or institutional discrimination possibly in the education system. Not to mention the

> discrimination they might receive from their peers before they would be confident about their background and therefore be able to assert themselves in terms of who they are and that they are not different from anybody. So they obviously have a need to develop good communication skills about themselves.
> *(Residential Social Worker)*

However, the fact that most social workers assumed cross-community children should be raised with one religious identity and almost one third of residential social workers suggested cross-community children did not face any particular needs, indicates this does not always happen in practice and is very much dependent on individual social workers' priorities. Only a small number of social workers described addressing cross-community identity issues with the children they work with on a one-to-one basis:

> I have gone out of my way and do sessions with him. I started on the basis of his very aggressive behaviour towards Catholic members of staff … I felt it was more deep rooted with him than some of the other kids … he had connections to the Loyalist organisations … I think with him it's just another way of venting his anger, if he knows someone is a Catholic he'll just go 'You Fenian whatever' but certainly there are small signs that he's taken some of it on board, he's not as aggressive towards some of the staff as he would have been … I think his feelings mainly stem from his community where he comes from and his knowledge of his father although he meets him on occasions the contact hasn't been sustained. He goes round to his father's house in a Catholic area, right on the fringe. It's also the area that he goes to throw stones, you know … I think basically he just sets his father aside from all that and goes on.
> *(Residential Social Worker)*

Indeed, surprisingly, some social workers were unaware children were from cross-community backgrounds prior to this research even though they were the key worker for those children.

> I wasn't aware that she came from a cross-community relationship. I've just done my first review for her, including a review of her file for here, and I came across no indication that there's a difference in religion.
> *(Residential Social Worker)*

> I wasn't even aware they were mixed and the foster parents were surprised about that as well.
> *(Field Social Worker)*

> You were saying she is from a mixed marriage background, you know, I mean no one had said to me and I looked at the files from her previous home. I'd be surprised if any other member of staff is aware of that.
> *(Residential Social Worker)*

Three social workers actually admitted they did not fulfil their legal obligation to promote the development of cross-community children's religious and cultural identity:

> I haven't a clue. I don't think we do it or see it. Cross-community is not seen as an identity.
> *(Field Social Worker)*

Some social workers indicated that individual social workers' perception of the importance of religion and whether or not religion is a private or public matter may impact on the priority they place on promoting a child's religious identity.

> It depends on how far down that road you are yourself and it's not really for social workers to be educating people about that … I wonder about how my personal view of religion influences it and maybe it's on forms because someone said it has to be but it's not prioritised – because outside of Northern Ireland how important is it?
> *(Field Social Worker)*

> The other issues are always a big priority and again so much depends I have to say on the individual social worker involved rather than the system itself, the system allows for it to be brought up, it's there on the form, if there's someone like myself who works with a church, and it's important to me but certainly I've been to reviews where I think to be

> honest at the moment I would say if a child isn't pushing it it's not an issue, in the majority. I would be more proactive because as a church goer myself it's important to me.
> *(Residential Social Worker)*

However, at the beginning of this report, it was noted that religious identity is directly linked to cultural and community identity in Northern Ireland. It impacts on where children can safely live, attend school, socialise and develop social relationships. Therefore, asking about religious identity cannot be discarded by social workers as simply a personal matter where they should not intervene. Rather, religious identity will impact on children's daily experiences and on the other needs outlined in the Children (NI) Order and associated procedures, such as education and social relationships. Social workers have a legal duty to meet the religious and cultural needs of children and must actively consider the impact of religious and cultural identity on the lives of looked after children from cross-community backgrounds.

Overall, many social workers felt they should be doing more to encourage children to pursue their religious and cultural interests. They felt this should be done in partnership with parents and children. Likewise, principal social workers emphasised the importance of consulting parents, addressing children's needs through the LAC (looked after children) process and maintaining children's attendance at religious and cultural events. However, they also assumed that in most cases cross-community children would follow one religious identity and therefore also assume a single community identity.

> I think the difficulty is trying to identify what religion or culture the child of the cross-community family adheres to … although their parents would be from two different communities, they would be from a particular community. I don't know of any young person who will appear to follow both faiths. And to be honest I'm not sure that's very helpful because young people need an identity. I mean there's only one school here that is an integrated school. So I would think the vast majority of our young people go to school to basically either a Catholic or Protestant school.
> *(Principal Social Worker)*

> Once we have identified the child is cross-community there's always the dominant and less dominant religion. With a single parent or an estranged partner we work with the

> parent caring for the child or the one who has a preference. If both parents are around and they disagree we look at what's available to meet the child's needs for example the geography, experience of the foster carer and whether the carer is from another religion.
> *(Principal Social Worker)*

Principal social workers suggested the LAC review process would monitor how children's religious and cultural needs were being met, although they acknowledged that it would not be a high priority in this reviewing process and could be overlooked because it is often assumed that carers are meeting the religious and cultural needs of children in their care.

> At LAC reviews as well there is a checklist although religion is not usually an issue. It would usually be about the care plan, contact, education and health issues. Religion is usually related to those things but it's not on the agenda.
> *(Principal Social Worker)*

> The children will probably fall into the practice in the way the foster parents unless if the parent is not happy with it. In residential care very few go to church. It's really the exception rather than the rule. Not because staff wouldn't go to, but children don't want to … You can't discuss everything at the review and at placement decisions so after that with foster parents you would leave a lot of it to them.
> *(Principal Social Worker)*

Principal social workers also acknowledged there were specific challenges for social workers trying to meet the needs of cross-community children. They emphasised the likelihood that these children are more likely to experience discrimination, changes to their religious identity, confusion about their identity and parental disagreements about their religious upbringing. Therefore, two principal social workers suggested that, although a policy for meeting the needs of cross-community children should not be devised, social work staff should become much more aware of the issues facing these children and their families:

> I'm thinking that we need to dig a bit deeper in a sense of what does cross-community mean for this specific child … You need to find out what are the views of the parents, so we

don't ostracise the child from a very important cultural identity or from a very important supportive network … You need to be very careful because each individual child has got subtleties and nuances that are only specific to that child and I think that's maybe what we need to look at highlighting but if you have a policy that says if you have this do this, that and the other it makes it very difficult, because in our work it's very rarely that we come across a case that is black and white.
(Principal Social Worker)

I think it's probably just a matter of emphasising for a lot of those areas in terms of ensuring that staff do address those issues. And maybe some kind of statement to ensure that staff don't forget about children from cross-community families. Clearly through this research if nothing else one of the things may well be the diversity of facts which means that staff need to be thinking about it a wee bit more than perhaps they have done in the past. I do believe really the LAC policies and procedures maybe could get a bit more focus on it than they have done.
(Principal Social Worker)

Assisting children who are changing religious identities

Since cross-community children were likely to change their religious identity, social workers were asked how they supported looked after children from cross-community backgrounds making such changes. Such support is particularly important in the Northern Irish context where altering religious identities would undoubtedly impact on children's cultural and community identity, including where they live or attend school. Four social workers found that these changes were often associated with children's feelings for each parent:

> I had a child who has changed. He blames his father who is a strong Republican and is not liked by the family. He befriended a gang – a peer group – of the opposite religious background to his father to rebel against him and now he's making sectarian remarks about Catholics. We ask him why

and seek to educate him but he's rebelling against his dad and can't articulate himself well. I hope dad gets the message.
(Residential Social Worker)

He had to find what's right for himself and his own feet … I mean he had that in his mind that he wanted to follow the father and it was the 'I'm the eldest son' thing. But he also had the mother chirping in his ear so I think in some ways the mother threw him into that by her physical abuse to him, him being removed from the household and having an opportunity to find himself and stand on his own two feet.
(Residential Social Worker)

Many social workers also suggested that children experienced peer pressure to change their religious identity. In addition, two social workers emphasised the impact of placement changes on the changing religious identity of looked after children:

He went to the local primary school which was a Catholic primary school because he lived in an area which was predominately Catholic and I suppose to a certain degree at that time that was influencing his life but he moved on and when he was living with granny then he went to a Protestant primary school and then the decision was made, which was a family decision, that he would go to the integrated college. It was at that stage … he had no Catholic influence at all because he was with granny and so he lost out. Had he stayed with the mother he would have gone to a Catholic school.
(Residential Social Worker)

Social workers suggested they would support children making such changes by listening to them, providing information and networking the child with their parents, clergy and other relevant professionals.

I would certainly look at why would they want to leave one religion and go to the other, let's look at the positive, and let's look at the negatives, we have to look at what would mum or dad say, whichever religion they're moving away from. I think it's when they're older they can make up their

> own mind and make decisions for themselves. What I would be looking at, perhaps is taking the young person is to a clergy of whatever religion they're going to, certainly the one they're coming away from and the one they're going to because there's different teachings in different churches and different things they have to find out, you know, helping them if they haven't found it out themselves.
> *(Field Social Worker)*

Social workers also emphasised that a key challenge for them would be dealing with family dynamics, especially when one or both parents disagree with the child's choice of religious identity.

> I would talk to them and [key child] has asked about Protestantism and I have taken her to my church to give her experience of a church. I got her hand-outs and literature and talked about the pros and cons and how others see it and if you would be a turncoat to your own family because children and young people don't think about the consequences or know about it.
> *(Residential Social Worker)*

> We would talk to the parents. When parents insist that we must fulfil the child's tradition it can be horrendous if the child doesn't want to and a strain on us as social workers who have to supervise. You begin to wonder whose needs are being met.
> *(Field Social Worker)*

However, three social workers recalled cases they had worked on when children had changed their religious identity and admitted that social workers did not undertake any individual or family work with the child at that time.

> Nothing was done with him when he returned to his family carers. There was no real discussion. I think they assumed he was young enough to accept the change.
> *(Field Social Worker)*

> That wasn't done for him but it should be done especially for children in care about the identity of each parent and where they are now because they could have a mishmash about the past, present or future.
> *(Female Field Social Worker)*

In addition, only one principal social worker felt the needs of children who made such changes were properly addressed.

Promoting anti-sectarianism

Both children and social workers highlighted important issues for cross-community children related to their experience of sectarianism. Social workers suggested they promoted anti-sectarianism by educating children and carers and by facilitating children's involvement in cross-community activities. Residential social work staff also explained they would immediately respond if a child acted in a sectarian manner by challenging their viewpoint, imposing sanctions and raising their awareness of prejudice. These social workers aimed to promote mutual understanding and respect between children of different religious and cultural backgrounds and some did not allow flaunting of cultural or political symbols within the residential home.

> The kids aren't allowed to display flags or banners in their rooms which would make other people feel uncomfortable. They are discouraged from playing the music which could be deemed sectarian … If they choose to wear those type of football tops they can but we don't and we advise them about safety issues. There would be a consequence for making sectarian comments or at least be made to sit down and talk through whatever it was that prompted these inappropriate outbursts. The children know if they are going to engage in that sort of behaviour there will be consequences. They are the ones that lose out.
> *(Residential Social Worker)*

However, several social workers emphasised that, depending on the area surrounding the home and the group of young people living there, promoting anti-sectarianism could be a real challenge and sometimes led to a situation where staff could only protect themselves:

> I mean for a lot of them it's just for the craic whatever is the teenage yobbish culture. It's nothing to do with the religion, not that they could tell you anyway … the group that we had last year were very violent, and if they wanted to riot you'd be on the doors, but what are you going to do? Stop them? You know, all you can do is report it. I don't know how any professional deals with that sort of very aggressive cultural sort. I think if there was one incident and it was isolated you could deal with it but not with that violence, you weren't dealing with it because you had maybe twelve or thirteen youths on your doorstep saying 'we know where you live'… it was just so overwhelming that nobody could, nobody would because you know, they weren't engaging, there was a real them and us environment. And you came in just hoping to get through your shift and go home. I mean they had stones pelting on the windows and the police had to get outside. There's no way I was going to go up to Johnny and say anything. It wasn't a children's home back then, you know … we were basically told to leave by the Loyalist organisations during the rioting and it was terrible, the kids were told that they were going to be burnt in their beds, by the young factions out there … they know that we are of mixed religion, so therefore we have Catholic children. But that's silly season for you … and it's very frightening. It was very stressful, we had a lot of different staff and staff refusing to come to work especially Catholic staff because they were being threatened.
> *(Residential Social Worker)*

> I think it's on a flare-up basis and they're just told off. It's not that well dealt with and would depend on individual staff members. Because the homes are mixed it is more tempting to spray walls with slogans and have flags to flaunt identity to other kids because of territory and status within the group.
> *(Field Social Worker)*

Several field social workers also discussed how entering areas where there are clear sectarian divisions sometimes made their work very difficult and threatened their own safety:

> You can find yourself in areas that it wouldn't matter what religion you are you wouldn't like to be in them. I have gone in one direction down a street and been taken into a room and asked who I was because people thought I was a policeman knocking on doors and I was actually looking for a house in the Republican area and was taken and had to prove who I was and I can tell you that wasn't very pleasant. I have also been threatened on the other side with 'You had better make sure that this boy gets it' [a favourable decision] particularly with a contact order … I have had two reminders of what would happen if things didn't go well. I got threatened by the LVF to make sure he gets contact in a decision there was no agreement on. That is much more than a religious issue.
> *(Field Social Worker)*

Principal social workers referred to house rules within residential children's homes such as banning offensive symbols. However, two principal social workers emphasised that it was very difficult to deal with sectarianism, especially when children were involved in sectarian riots or exhibiting sectarian attitudes and actions.

> There used to be the Apprentice Boy march when there was a serious riot, that was a very difficult situation because it was caught between two housing estates, one Nationalist Republican, the other Protestant Loyalist and we were literally in the interface between the two of them which was a major problem.
> *(Principal Social Worker)*

> You have to understand this sectarian stuff is becoming a really big issue. I think we are seeing evidence of young people where paramilitaries are targeting young people so we have children now in children's homes who are part of these groups! Children are threatening staff with paramilitary strikes so we need to have contacts to ask them to leave us alone. We struggle with those things like flags and emblems and trying to get children to understand the issues. It is getting tougher. I think we have not done this in a good way and we need to be more organised. It is more

> complicated now. We have been talking with managers and meeting with heads of units every month and our intention is to try and help staff to deal with it. We have to look after the children. I think it is a big of a struggle at the minute.
> *Interviewer: What guidance do social workers have on how to deal with that?*
> We're scratching our heads
> *(Principal Social Worker)*

Almost half of all the social workers interviewed (14 out of 31) felt inadequately skilled to deal with issues related to sectarianism. Those social workers (17 out of 31) who did feel they were adequately skilled referred to their ability to be critically reflexive, their work experience, training and personal experience of living in Northern Ireland.

> The formal training through the social work and within the Trust would be very good and I think it helps with the experience you do build up as well. I have worked in various areas that are regarded as having difficulties with sectarianism and at times there is little substitute for experience when dealing with all the stresses and strains.
> *(Field Social Worker)*

> It's one of those things that we all think we're probably not very sectarian people and I suppose it points out to us that we have to examine our practices. I would say that I'm skilled because I'm open to criticism and if somebody can point out to me look that particular way of working with a child is sectarian or discriminatory or whatever and hopefully I'm big enough to say I've been blind to my own prejudice and look into it and see what can I do about it.
> *(Residential Social Worker)*

> It's no more than you deal with yourself living in Northern Ireland.
> *(Field Social Worker)*

Those who felt they were not adequately skilled suggested there was little they could do to effectively challenge the influence of widespread sectarianism. They felt more appropriate training on dealing with sectarian issues was required. Even social workers who had not experienced an incident where they had to deal with sectarianism were unsure how they would deal with such a situation if it arose in the future.

> On a professional level, no, because if there were specific ways of dealing with things I would like to be trained to provide me with more knowledge and that information for dealing with decisions like that.
> *(Residential Social Worker)*

> I don't think anybody does because it is such a political climate and no one has solutions. You just advise and guide children but there's very little you can do to stop it … I do think going on a course is not enough. I think all training should include that.
> *(Field Social Worker)*

In addition, more than half of the residential social workers interviewed felt that other colleagues were inadequately skilled to deal with sectarianism. These social workers expressed concern that some staff were not adequately trained, were reluctant to openly discuss issues relating to sectarianism or allowed their own belief systems to influence their work:

> I had my eyes opened and I was shocked at that experience of the anti-sectarianism training. When it came down to the nitty-gritty of challenging attitudes, prejudices that people have, rather than go through that themselves they decided to say 'I'm not going to do that'. They were a bit challenged to find themselves trying to overcome that. I've never felt uncomfortable with any of that at all.
> *(Residential Social Worker)*

> I think we all are dealing with it and I think it depends on some people if they are really into their religion and very strong in their beliefs then it can be more difficult to teach open mindedly.
> *(Residential Social Worker)*

They emphasised that it was important that staff were open to criticism and willing to receive support and information from other colleagues.

> ... we have a good team spirit here and we hope we can accept criticism at a professional level. And I think that staff here would be strong enough to challenge each other on the times we haven't and advocate for children with other members of staff.
> *(Residential Social Worker)*

Social workers suggested they ensured that foster carers promoted anti-sectarianism in their care of children by having open discussions with carers, liasing with their link worker from the foster care team and addressing situations where children begin to develop sectarian attitudes.

> That would be looked at in training and assessment of carers. We would make them aware of their needs and ensure they are prepared to allow them to follow their own paths and not make them feel uncomfortable about that. We would ask them to make sure those issues can be talked about with no difficulty. We would talk to children and look at foster parents' actions like if they were opposed to a child joining a particular club or something like that.
> *(Field Social Worker)*

However, social workers acknowledged that some carers were sectarian and it was difficult to challenge their attitudes:

> That's very difficult, because some of our carers are not anti-sectarian and are sectarian. And that means that the culture of their home is quite sectarian.
> *(Field Social Worker)*

> Through training and it is possible they would be sectarian and it's difficult to change that. They are brought up with that and it's easy to impart that onto the child. If young people are not comfortable then that has to be nipped in the bud and the child may have to be moved on because it could be detrimental.
> *(Field Social Worker)*

Several social workers were unsure how they would address a situation where a carer is not promoting anti-sectarianism:

> That's difficult. I don't know – maybe we bring up religious or political views and not sectarianism. We would talk and not challenge. If they do something that is sectarian I would inform them in a safe way but if it continually comes up I'm not sure how we address that properly.
> *(Field Social Worker)*

Principal social workers acknowledged there are not any specific policies or guidance for social workers on how to ensure carers promote anti-sectarianism in their care of children. However, they suggested that promoting anti-sectarianism within anti-discriminatory practice is an integral part of the ethos of professional social work.

> I don't think any specific guidance as such, but you know the whole ethos of social work would be to challenge anti-discriminatory practice and sectarian practice, so certainly that would be part of the professional duties of the social workers … We would have to be speaking to the child and … challenging the carers in relation to that.
> *(Principal Social Worker)*

> I can't honestly say that we make particular reference to that in our policy and guidance … we have had certain concerns ourselves with some of our foster carers who have particularly strong political views … I think that with regard to those issues we put it to one side and really avoid it and the uncomfortable feelings that go along with it … we all have our different views about things and maybe some of us would be better keeping them down there somewhere rather than bring them up to the surface. We have staff who we know have had particularly strong political views which some of us have a struggle to agree with … and how do you reconcile these sorts of issues for staff and for carers? We've tried to offer guidance at a verbal level but there's nothing in writing saying 'Here's how we think you should try and manage this one'… it's a very sensitive issue. We have talked to foster carers about this and our staff have found that difficult before …
> *(Principal Social Worker)*

Training opportunities for social workers and carers

Only two out of the 31 social workers had received training on meeting the religious and cultural needs of looked after children. None of the social workers had received training on meeting the needs of cross-community children. Some social workers felt that meeting the religious and cultural needs of looked after children may have been an integral part of training on other issues or new legislation such as the Human Rights Act. However, they felt attention to that particular subject would have been minimal and would not have addressed the needs of looked after children who come from cross-community families. Indeed, addressing religious, cultural or sectarian issues was an area that the majority of social workers felt was not properly addressed in their social work or post-qualifying training. Most of the social workers would like to participate in training on meeting the religious and cultural needs of looked after children and the needs of cross-community children.

> We had one or two lectures on the course but it was very badly done. I think the group need to know each other because it was getting people's backs up and was actually creating sectarian tensions.
> *(Field Social Worker)*

> I did go to a training session on anti-sectarianism and anti-discriminatory practice. The sad thing from that, to be quite honest, was that the wrong kind of person was running it. When we had those sessions in-house people's attitudes were tested, you know some people were so engrained in their culture and weren't prepared to continue ... So within the team it is not at all discussed, we didn't like talking about this thing and we avoided the question ... because when it comes to colleagues you don't really know them and you don't know what baggage they carry but you need to say and think about it.
> *(Residential Social Worker)*

> I have never been involved in it – I've never seen it in the training manual or anything, actually it was flagged up on our last training day – how people feel inadequate with

> regarding cultural background and stuff … that's very relevant in my job today … We're only getting our heads around that now with the peace process but sectarianism would be a big issue for us. You might get one hour training sessions but a lot is left with you and you might not cover it at all if you didn't pick that topic for an essay.
> **(Residential Social Worker)**

Interestingly, one social worker felt she did not require any training on these issues because she did not believe cross-community children had any particular needs:

> I've never looked at them as specifically cross-community. I've been a social worker for twenty-two years. I think an awful lot of it is your own common sense, your own understanding, I think living in Northern Ireland and you get to know all the things that are the flashpoints that surround the kids. I think a lot of that is you being sensitive towards people's feelings and their opinions. I don't think you need an awful lot of training, since I'm a mother myself and I would know a lot of what kids need. I mean they know what we are, end of story, but it's not in our conversations all the time, and taking kids into care sometimes you wouldn't even know.
> **(Field Social Worker)**

The majority of foster carers had been offered training. This training dealt with a wide range of issues: challenging behaviour, child sexual abuse, child development, homelessness, mental health, drug use, attachment, legislation and child protection. However, only one foster carer indicated they had received training on anti-sectarian or anti-discriminatory practice. None of the foster carers had received training on meeting the religious and cultural needs of children or meeting the needs of cross-community children, although more than half of the carers interviewed would like to access training on these issues.

> Definitely like training. We've been foster parents for twenty-six years but times and children change. You have to be aware and now with all the red tape you have to watch your back and it's only fair to the child to be aware.
> **(Carer)**

Those who did not wish to participate in training on those issues felt they did not have time, they were already adequately skilled from their experience of rearing other children or they preferred not to raise issues related to religion in Northern Ireland.

> I was offered training but I didn't accept them … I had no training to rear my own and I do everything for my own as I do for them. Maybe at the start I would have liked to but I steer clear now unless it's compulsory. We are their parents now so I would only ask the social worker if there were problems.
> *(Carer)*

> In the early days I was so busy and just getting on with it but the ones I went to were very useful. Maybe if you don't look for a problem you don't find it or there is none. Religion isn't talked about in this house.
> *(Carer)*

Principal social workers also commented on the provision of training for staff and carers on meeting the religious and cultural needs of looked after children and, in particular, those from cross-community backgrounds. Reflecting the views of social work staff, principal social workers felt that, although it may have been generally covered through training on other subjects, no specific training or guidance was available.

> Our training team deal with this and checking through 2000–2001 training programme it's not on that at all. I do think it was identified, mind you, as an issue in the Social Services Inspectorate foster care report … we've certainly identified that through to our trainers as something that might be incorporated in with a training programme in the future. There's training for foster carers and there's sixty-six courses listed here within the family childcare programme. I don't see one specifically counting as religious or cultural needs. Sometimes it's not possible to get everything into the training agenda but I think there was something of an issue there. And certainly staff need teaching on things like when they're talking to children in those circumstances how are children dealing with that and coping with it.
> *(Principal Social Worker)*

They felt that foster carers required specific training on meeting the religious and cultural needs of looked after children in general and meeting the needs of cross-community children in particular.

> Things are inadequate with the foster carer training agenda at present anyway generally speaking because of staffing and funding issues. But I think we do need to put together more comprehensive training programmes for foster carers. And in particular carers who have been asked to care for children not necessarily from their own background. I'm not sure that we have really addressed that one at all and certainly there's a gap there and a need for an overall audit. We are required to do annual reviews of foster carers, and one of the questions is what are the training needs of these foster carer … I think we need to be doing proper reviews and … checking out have they received it. If they haven't we should be giving them a training programme … and take that forward.
> *(Principal Social Worker)*

Principal social workers also admitted that the Trust did not provide comprehensive training for carers on promoting anti-sectarianism in their care of children. Indeed, they reported limited training for foster carers in general.

Summary

Findings suggest that looked after children from cross-community backgrounds often experienced confusion about their religious identity and felt pressurised to either disguise their mixed identity or choose one religious identity. Decisions about religious identity for cross-community children who were looked after were highly influenced by the religious background of their carer, their contact with both sides of their birth family and the location of their placement. Comments children made suggest that although children preferred to maintain a cross-community identity they found this very difficult because educational, housing and social spaces were segregated. They were also pressurised to choose one religion by their parents and peers. Indeed, many social workers and carers assumed cross-community children should choose one religious identity and identify with one community background. Social workers suggested they would support and advise children who decided to change their religious identity, however, they described specific cases where children had made such changes and neither carers nor social workers had discussed the dynamics of this process with the child. Additionally, some foster carers and social workers were unaware that children in their care were from a cross-community background before their involvement in this study.

Comments from social workers and foster carers who discussed how they promoted children's religious and cultural identities indicated that they usually focused on attendance at religious ceremonies only. Indeed, some carers admitted they preferred to avoid discussions about religion and community background and some social workers suggested that their views on religion would detrimentally influence their professional efforts to promote children's religious identity. Despite this, most foster carers felt adequately skilled to meet the religious and cultural needs of cross-community children and were pleased that social services did not prioritise promoting children's religious needs. Likewise, most social workers claimed they did not prioritise promoting children's religious and cultural needs because of resource constraints and other priorities.

Living in a segregated society increased the likelihood that cross-community children would experience discrimination and sectarianism, especially when they lived in homes close to interface areas. Some social workers made efforts to address sectarianism, for example by educating children and sanctioning sectarian actions. However, more than half of the social workers surveyed felt inadequately skilled to deal with sectarianism and described tense situations where staff felt at risk. Indeed, some social workers were concerned about colleagues' reluctance to address anti-oppressive issues. Only a very small number of social workers or carers had received training on meeting the religious or cultural needs of children and none had received training on the particular needs of cross-community children. Many social workers suggested that more training and awareness-raising was required for staff and carers to ensure they were able to critically reflect on their own practice.

8. Space for everyone: improving services for cross-community families

The findings from this research show that cross-community children and their families living in Northern Ireland have particular experiences and needs because of their mixed identity. The data presented in previous chapters raise concerns about the efforts social workers make to meet the religious and cultural needs of these children when they become looked after. This chapter summarises the core findings of the study and makes suggestions for the development of policy and practice that should more effectively meet the needs of these children and their families.

Meeting the needs of cross-community families in Northern Ireland

It is clear from the findings presented, that cross-community families living in Northern Ireland face a range of discriminatory barriers. These include dealing with negative family and public attitudes towards cross-community relationships and finding it difficult to access neutral, safe areas. In the context of a divided and violent society, these families are under pressure to choose one religious identity or keep their dual identity secret. Indeed, they are also more likely to experience sectarian intimidation and violence. The crucial decisions parents of cross-community children make are influenced by all of these factors and are restricted by the persistent segregation of educational systems, housing areas and social structures. Generally, cross-community parents believe that these additional stressors have a detrimental effect on their ability to maintain strong family relationships and care for their children.

Given these circumstances, the importance of providing effective support services for cross-community families cannot be underestimated. Although the majority of cross-community parents in this study did not feel that being cross-community was the main reason for their contact with social services, they acknowledged the critical effects of these additional stressors and the lack of accessible community support systems. Other researchers have noted the importance of family and community networks as sources of informal social support, especially when families feel threatened (McAuley and Kremer 1990). However, half of the parents of children in need and three quarters of the parents of looked after children were dissatisfied with the support services available when they began to experience difficulties. The findings indicate that these families require more accessible support services based in local, neutral and safe communities. In addition, existing support services tailored to meet the needs of cross-community families, such as NIMMA (Northern Ireland Mixed Marriage Association), also require further development and expansion to provide a greater diversity of services and increase accessibility for more families across Northern Ireland.

Aside from the need to provide support services for cross-community parents, children from cross-community backgrounds also have specific needs. Given the divided nature of Northern Irish society they often live in segregated communities, attend segregated schools and participate in segregated social activities. This limits the opportunities these children have to access integrated spaces or meet others from both religious backgrounds. Such segregation also increases pressure on cross-community children to conform with the dominant religion in their immediate environment or to disguise their dual identity. Most children involved in this study were deeply aware of other people's negative attitudes towards cross-community families and the risk of sectarian discrimination or violence targeted against them.

Consideration of cross-community identity

Despite descriptions from cross-community parents and children about their particular experiences and needs, the majority of social workers in this study still believed this group of children do not face significant issues. Even when social workers did recognise their particular experiences, there was an overall reluctance to seriously consider their needs.

Fundamentally, social workers require knowledge about children's backgrounds to be able to help children develop a sense of identity and to devise care plans that meet their religious and cultural needs. However, social workers in this study revealed limited knowledge about children's cross-community backgrounds. A major concern is the finding that more than half the social workers interviewed admitted children's religious identities were often assumed. This may be because social workers find it difficult to consult parents and children about their religious identity. This was especially challenging when families held strong political or sectarian beliefs, made assumptions about social workers' religious identity or could not decide about their children's religious identity.

For cross-community children who became looked after, the location of their placement and the carer's background had a direct influence on their religious and cultural upbringing. Furthermore, community divisions and conflicting cultural and political beliefs influenced the contact cross-community children had with their family. In addition, many of the looked after children from cross-community backgrounds in this study changed their religious and cultural identity in accordance with their placement or contact with one side of their birth family. In the context of Northern Ireland, this shift has significant implications for children as it impacts on all areas of their lives including their community identity, social relationships and personal safety. However, social workers often failed to address these issues with children who had made such changes.

Social workers usually assumed cross-community children should choose one religious identity to fit into Northern Irish society. However, good anti-discriminatory social work practice would suggest that cross-community children should be offered choices about their identity that account for their cross-community background, their feelings towards each birth parent and their perceptions of their religious and cultural identity. Therefore, promoting a positive self-identity for cross-community children requires understanding of their bi-cultural family background, consideration of their place in society and a firm commitment to maintaining appropriate contact with cultural and familial support networks (Masson 1997; Gilligan 2000; Dutt and Phillips 2000). Thoburn (1994) suggested the promotion of self-identity requires skilled social work intervention. However, social workers in this study revealed limited knowledge about children's family background and minimal efforts to address the complex identity needs of cross-community children. Indeed, in some cases social workers were unaware that children they worked with were from cross-community backgrounds.

Reflecting findings from previous studies, it appears there is a general lack of clarity among social workers and carers about how to assist these children to develop a positive self-concept within a divided society (Robinson 1992; Morgan *et al.* 1996; Leitch and Kilpatrick 1999; McCay and Sinclair 1999). Some social workers indicated they perceived decisions about religious identity within the context of a divided society as a sensitive and private matter. However, it is clear that decisions about religion can be so closely tied to cultural identity that they cannot be so simply dismissed. Identity is recognised as one of the seven dimensions of children's developmental needs (DH 1995; DHSS (NI) 1996). For children living in Northern Ireland identity impacts on other facets of their developmental needs, such as education, safe housing or family and social relationships. For looked after children in Northern Ireland, decisions about their religious upbringing are related to where they live, which school they attend, the community they belong to, their social relationships and their contact with family members. All of these issues are essential factors to be considered in care plans for looked after children.

Legislation demands that social workers actively seek to meet children's religious and cultural needs. Therefore, it is not acceptable to ignore these needs. While it may be much more difficult to meet these needs in the context of a sectarian and sometimes violent society this then is the challenge that social workers and their managers face: to address the impact of such divisions on children's identity and social work practice. Methods for promoting positive community relations, self-identity and addressing sectarianism have been outlined in previous literature (Smyth 1994; Morrow and Wilson 1996; Fairmichael 1997; Playboard 1997; Community Relations Council 1997; CCETSW 1999; Connolly 1999). It is crucial that such methods are adopted by social workers in their work with looked after children, especially those from cross-community backgrounds who are likely to experience discrimination and identity confusion.

Experience of sectarian discrimination and segregation has a profound effect on the identity of looked after children who come from cross-community backgrounds. These children felt pressurised to choose one identity to fit in with either community or to deny one parent's background. However, social workers felt that addressing sectarian issues presented significant personal and professional challenges. The majority of social workers were unaware of anti-discriminatory or anti-sectarian policies and felt inadequately skilled to deal with tense sectarian situations. Indeed, it seemed that some social workers were unwilling to address anti-sectarian issues. These findings highlight the urgent need for more effective training and awareness-raising for staff and carers with support from managers to ensure they critically reflect on their practice. This is a serious training need since many social workers, especially residential social workers, struggle with the sectarian issues facing children and young people in their care. Authors have repeatedly emphasised the need for a more radical social work approach that more effectively promotes anti-sectarianism and positive community relations, however findings from this study seem to suggest little has changed (Thompson 1993; Diamond and Godfrey 1997; Smyth and Campbell 1996; Traynor 1998).

Meeting the needs of cross-community children in public care

Three main themes emerge from the data related to meeting the needs of cross-community children in public care. These are placement choices, identity needs and family contact.

As noted in previous research, social workers in this study emphasised that resource constraints restricted placement choices and impacted on care planning (McAuley 2000; DHSS/SSI (NI) 2000). As a result, social workers prioritised the immediate safety needs of children and placed their religious and cultural needs as a low priority. This meant that social workers did not consider the influence of placement decisions on children's religious identity and family relationships, especially when siblings had different religious and cultural upbringing. This situation was further exacerbated when parents felt they had little input into decisions about their child's religious and cultural identity. Given the level of sectarian division in Northern Ireland, simply placing a child in a particular area in effect impacts on their religious, cultural and community identity and their personal safety. It will influence which schools children attend, the religious and cultural background of friends and the contact children have with their birth family. For cross-community children, it will also influence which part of their dual religious and cultural background they may feel pressurised to reject or hide. This ultimately has repercussions for children's relationships with that side of their family. For example, these findings illustrate children usually only maintain contact with external family members from one side of their bi-cultural background, usually the most dominant family side or those that matched the child's religious identity. Social workers and carers may also unintentionally influence the child's religious and cultural identity, although others were wary of inadvertently exerting influence that overshadowed the wishes and feelings of their birth parents.

Different identity issues arose for children living in foster care from those living in residential care. The key issue for children in foster placements was the ability of their carer to provide them with information and experience of their bi-cultural family and community background and where possible maintain contact with both sides of their birth family. Since these children are more likely to experience confusion, discrimination and changes to their identity, it is crucial that carers create an environment for open communication about religious and cultural identity and equip them with the language and skills to deal with sectarian experiences. Social workers also need to feel adequately skilled to address these issues openly with carers and ensure that carers adopt such approaches in their care of cross-community children. Even when social workers and carers felt they were addressing children's religious and cultural needs they usually focused solely on attendance at religious ceremonies. There was little consideration of the relevance of religious identity to cultural and community identity and minimal efforts to address cross-community children's experience of sectarianism. Indeed, due to the segregated and conflictual nature of Northern Irish society, some carers preferred to avoid discussions about religion and politics. In addition, social workers admitted that their personal views on religion sometimes detrimentally affected their professional efforts to promote children's religious and cultural identities.

The same issues are relevant for residential social work practice. However, children living in residential care also experienced additional challenges, as they were more likely to experience peer pressure to choose the dominant religion of others living in the home or the community area in which the home is sited. Cross-community children seemed to learn effective ways of disguising or adapting their religious identity as they move between segregated spaces. However, more attention must be paid to the effects of this pressure – to constantly re-negotiate and reconstruct identity, in accordance with situational and contextual shifts – on children's sense of community belonging. Residential social workers provided many examples of the complex issues cross-community children in residential care faced, including safety issues for children crossing violent interface areas and their involvement in local rioting. However, they were unsure how to effectively address these issues with cross-community children. In accordance with current legislative duties and the ethos of anti-sectarian practice, social workers in Northern Ireland need to be skilled to deal with these specific issues for looked after children from cross-community backgrounds.

The usual family contact difficulties that are applicable to all looked after children, such as practical constraints, were further accentuated for cross-community families. For example, geographical distance became more complex for cross-community children whose parents had separated as they often moved back to opposite community areas where contact may be unsafe for children.

The dynamics of family contact may be difficult for any looked after child. However, for cross-community children whose parents come from different religious and cultural backgrounds this can be more complicated. Parents may disagree with each other or their child about religious and cultural upbringing, especially when family members held strong political beliefs. This can then affect children's relationships with one or both parents. Separated parents may also form new relationships with partners. This can create problems for looked after children from cross-community backgrounds, especially if they return to the care of a birth parent and step-parent who have a different religious and cultural identity.

Developing policy and practice

Findings from this study clearly indicate services to support cross-community children and their families need to be improved. This need for more effective support services is not only applicable to social workers but also to other professionals and agencies that provide services for children and their families, particularly housing. Making more efforts to support these families in the community may prevent the over-representation of these children in the public care system in Northern Ireland. From the findings of this study, it is possible to make suggestions for the development of policy and practice to improve efforts to meet the religious and cultural needs of looked after children in general and, in particular, to meet the needs of looked after children from cross-community backgrounds. These suggestions can be discussed under three key themes: space for everyone; cross-community children in public care; and promoting anti-sectarian practice.

Space for everyone

In the context of Northern Ireland, cross-community children and their families face difficulties related to rejection, isolation, discrimination and intimidation. This does not mean that cross-community relationships will inevitably be unsuccessful. In contrast, the difficulties cross-community families experience are a result of external barriers imposed by family members, the local community, societal attitudes and service providers. When these barriers are overcome cross-community children and their families have many positive experiences of their dual identity that should be celebrated.

However, these families find it difficult to access neutral, integrated support services. Services are either inaccessible; seen only to serve those of a particular community background; or service providers are uninformed about the particular needs of cross-community families. Indeed, families of looked after children believed that if appropriate services had been available for their family their child may not have entered public care. Overall, cross-community families did not indicate that they required unique services. They wanted access to services that any family in the community may require such as counselling, advice on effective parenting and safe social activities for their children. These families need space in the community where their dual identity is accepted and access to services where staff are aware and accepting of the diversity of parental backgrounds and are sensitive to their needs. Based on these findings, there are four key areas that should be developed to improve support services available to these families in the community. There is a need to:

- establish and develop accessible and local services in neutral areas

- aim to provide a range of integrated services (such as schools, mother and toddler groups, after-school clubs, family centres, housing) accessible to both sides of the community rather than segregated services in divided communities

- raise awareness of the needs of cross-community families among service providers in the community (Family Policy Unit of the DHSSPS and voluntary organisations, such as the Parents' Advice Centre, could address the support needs of parents of cross-community children)

- support the development of existing organisations in the community that provide services for cross-community families (such as NIMMA) and network cross-community families in need to these services.

Cross-community children in public care

Effective implementation of the Children (NI) Order 1995 concerning the religious and cultural needs of children will require recognition of the particular needs of cross-community children who are over-represented in public care in Northern Ireland. Religious and cultural identity needs impact on other areas of children's lives such as education and safety. However, findings from this research indicate that social workers do not acknowledge or prioritise these needs. Ignoring the importance of identity within other aspects of children's developmental needs has a detrimental impact on the experiences of cross-community children in public care. Therefore, it is suggested that social workers should:

- increase their understanding of the experiences and needs of cross-community children

- consult with children and their families about children's religious and cultural upbringing and the child's wishes and feeling about this

- prioritise the identity needs of cross-community children

- take time to consider the religious and cultural needs of cross-community children when making important choices about their lives, for example concerning placements and family contact

- promote positive cross-community religious and cultural identities in accordance with current legal duties, including acceptance and support for dual identities

- develop awareness of the impact of religious and cultural identity on children's developmental needs and family relationships

- recognise that religious and cultural needs in the context of Northern Ireland go beyond attendance at services to include issues of spiritual, cultural, community and political aspects of religious identity

- record more accurate and comprehensive information relating to the religious and cultural identity of children, including records of both birth parents' backgrounds, in order to inform and support effective care planning for these looked after children.

Promoting anti-sectarian practice

Social workers raised issues relating to the promotion of anti-sectarian practice at two levels. First, there was a lack of clarity on how to support children who experience sectarian discrimination, how to educate children to keep them safe and how to advise foster carers. Second, sectarianism impacted on social workers' relationships with colleagues as well as families and in some situations social workers became targets for sectarianism. For example, some social workers had been threatened by representatives of paramilitary groups. Social workers were unsure about how they should respond to such situations in accordance with current legislation. It is clear from this research that social work staff and foster carers require further guidance and training on how to address the impact of sectarianism on their own practice and the discrimination cross-community children are likely to experience.

Education and post-qualifying training will need to advance existing social work knowledge and skills within the anti-oppressive ethos of social work practice. Previous literature has outlined techniques for parents, carers and professionals to address sectarianism that could inform such training strategies (Smyth 1994; Morrow and Wilson 1996; Fairmichael 1997; Playboard 1997; Community Relations Council 1997; Connolly 1999). Indeed, CCETSW (1999) outlined specific training and practice guidelines for staff within the Personal Social Services sector. Findings from this study suggest that staff training should seek to develop:

- understanding of the effects of sectarianism
- critical self-awareness
- skills for working across sectarian boundaries
- methods for applying anti-sectarian policies to practice
- commitment to equal opportunities regardless of religious or cultural background.

In addition, practitioners promoting positive community relations and an active anti-sectarian approach will need practical and emotional support from managers who value such approaches. Practitioners will also require adequate resources and a firm commitment to anti-sectarianism to overcome fear, avoidance and apathy at individual and institutional levels.

Conclusion

The primary aims of this research were to examine the needs and experiences of cross-community children and their families, to ascertain how these were being addressed by social services and to explore the reasons why these children are over-represented in public care in Northern Ireland. Findings from the study have fulfilled these aims by providing knowledge about the experiences of cross-community families and the services they received. The research also begins to address the dearth of literature on the views of cross-community children and provides evidence-based suggestions for the improvement of services to meet their religious and cultural needs. Cross-community children are a substantial group with the public care system and since the numbers of cross-community relationships appear to be increasing, the onus on service providers to respond to their needs will become more difficult to ignore. Given that cross-community children are over-represented in the public care system in Northern Ireland, it is vital that social workers develop understanding of their needs. Fulfilling the legal requirement to assess and then plan to meet the religious and cultural needs of each individual looked after child, within a holistic anti-sectarian approach, can only enhance the service provided to cross-community children.

References

Alibhai-Brown, J and Montague, A (1992) *The Colour of Love*. Virago

Bagnall, A, Heery, G, McConkey, W, Pinkerton, J and Smyth, M eds (1995) *Difference, Diversity and Discrimination*. Northern Ireland Post-Qualifying and Training Partnership

Banks, N (1992) Some Considerations of Racial Identification and Self-Esteem When Working with Mixed Ethnicity Children and their Mothers as Social Services Clients, *Social Services Research*, 3, 32–41

Barn, R, Sinclair, R and Ferninand, D (1997) *Acting on Principle: An Examination of Race and Ethnicity in Social Services Provision for Children and Families*. BAAF

Bebbington, A and Miles, J (1989) The Background of Children who are in Local Authority Care, *British Journal of Social Work*, 19, 5

Bricher, G (1999) Children and Qualitative Research Methods: A Review of the Literature Related to Interview and Interpretive Processes. *Nurse Researcher*, 6, 4, 65–77

Brewer, J (1992) The Parallels between Sectarianism and Racism: The Northern Ireland Experience In One Small Step Towards Racial Justice: The Teaching of Anti-Racism in Diploma in Social Work Programmes, *Improving Social Education and Training* 8, CCETSW

Byrne, S (1997) *Growing up in a Divided Society: The Influence of Conflict on Belfast Schoolchildren*. New Jersey: Fairleigh Dickinson University Press

Cairns, E (1987) *Caught in the Crossfire: Children and the Northern Ireland Conflict*. Appletree Press

Cairns, E (1996) *Children and political conflict*. Blackwell

Central Council for Education and Training in Social Work (CCETSW) (NI) (1999) *Getting Off the Fence: Challenging Sectarianism in Personal Social Services*. CCETSW (NI)

Community Relations Council (1997) *Games Not Names: Play and Community Relations*. Playboard and Community Relations Council

Connolly, P (1997) *Sectarianism, children and cross-community contact schemes: a study of 10 and 11 year old children's perspectives in Northern Ireland*. Paper presented to the British Educational Research Association Annual Conference 11–14 September, University of York

Connolly, P (1999) *Community Relations Work with Preschool Children*. Community Relations Council

Connolly, P and Maginn, P (1999) *Sectarianism, Children and Community Relations in Northern Ireland*. Centre for the Study of Conflict, University of Ulster

Connolly, P, Smith, A and Kelly, B (2002) *Too Young to Notice? The Cultural and Political Awareness of 3–6 Year Olds in Northern Ireland*. Community Relations Council

Department of Health (1995) *Looking After Children Materials*. HMSO

Department of Health and Social Services (NI) (1996) *Looking After Children Materials*. The Stationery Office

DHSS/SSI (NI) (2000) *Planning to Care: An Overview Report of Care Planning for Children Subject to Statutory Intervention in Northern Ireland*, Belfast: DHSS/SSI (NI)

Diamond, A and Godfrey, A (1997) The Children (NI) Order: Understanding Social Diversity and Challenging Oppression, *Child Placement in Practice*, 5, 1

Dominelli, L (1988) *Anti-Racist Social Work*. Macmillan

Dutt, R and Phillips, M Assessing black children in need and their families *in Assessing Children in Need and their Families: Practice Guidance* (2000). TSO

Fairmichael, R (1997) *A Skills Guide for Community Relations Work in Northern Ireland*. Community Relations Council

Farmer, E and Owen, M (1995) *Child Protection Practice: Private Risks and Public Remedies*. HMSO

Finlay, A Reflexivity and the Dilemmas of Identification: An Ethnographic Encounter in Northern Ireland, pp 55-76 *in* Smyth, M and Robinson, G eds (2001) *Researching Violently Divided Societies: Ethical and Methodological Issues*. Pluto Press

Fitzduff, M and Frazer, H (1986) *Improving Community Relations*. Standing Advisory Committee on Human Rights

Fraser, M (1973) *Children in conflict*. Secker and Warburg

Geraghty, T (1999) *Getting it Right? The State of Children's Rights in Northern Ireland at the end of the 20th Century*. Children's Law Centre

Gilligan, R (2000) The Key Role of Social Workers in Promoting the Well-Being of Children in State Care – A Neglected Dimension of Reforming Policies, *Children and Society*, 14, 4, 267–76

Glendinning, W (2001) *Mixed Marriages: The International Dimension*. Conference Proceedings, 26–27 November 2001, Belfast

Harbison, J ed. (1983) *Children of the Troubles: Children in Northern Ireland*. Stranmillis College, Learning Resources Unit

Harter, S. (1985) *Manual for the Self-Perception Profile for Children.* Denver: University of Denver

Hill, M (1997) *Participatory Research with Children Child and Family Social Work,* 2, 3, 171–183

Holliday, L (1997) *Children of 'The Troubles': Our Lives in the Crossfire of Northern Ireland.* New York: Pocket Books

Horgan, G and Sinclair, R (1997) *Planning for Children in Care in Northern Ireland.* National Children's Bureau

Hughes, J and Donnelly, C (2001) Integrate or Segregate? Ten Years of Social Attitudes to Community Relations in Northern Ireland, *Northern Ireland Life and Times Survey,* Research Update Number 9

Jarman, N and O'Halloran, C (2001) Recreational Rioting: Young People, Interface Areas and Violence, *Child Care in Practice,* 7, 1, 2–16

Joseph, S, Cairns, E and McCollam, P (1993) Political Violence, Coping, and Depressive Symptomatology in Northern Irish Children, *Personality and Individual Differences,* 15, 4, 471–3

Katz, I (1996) *Social Construction of a Mixed Parentage Identity: Mixed Metaphor.* Jessica Kingsley Publishers

Kelly, B (2002) Young People's Views on Communities and Sectarianism in Northern Ireland, *Child Care in Practice,* 8, 1, 65–73

Kelly, B, McColgan, M and Scally, M (2000) 'A Chance to Say' – Involving Children who have Learning Disabilities in a Pilot Study on Family Support Services, *Journal of Learning Disabilities for Nursing, Health and Social Care,* 4 ,2, 115–27

Lampen, J (1995) *Building the Peace: Good practice in community relations work in Northern Ireland.* Community Relations Council

Lee, R L (1994) *Class, Ethnicity, Mixed and Matched: Interreligious Courtship and Marriage in Northern Ireland.* Gender and the Democratic Union Volume 2. London: University Press of America

Leitch, R and Kilpatrick, R (1999) *Inside the Gates: Schools and the Troubles.* Save the Children

Levy, A (2000) The Human Rights Act 1998: The Implications for Children, *Child Care in Practice,* 6, 3, 289-94

MacDonald, S (1991) *All Equal Under the Act.* National Institute for Social Work

Masson, J (1997) Maintaining contact between parents and children in the public care, *Children and Society,* 11, 4, 222–30

McAuley, C (1996) *Children in Long-Term Foster Care: Emotional and Social Development*. Aldershot: Avebury Press

McAuley, C (2000) Safeguarding children: placement choice and creating a vision for looked after children in Northern Ireland, *Adoption and Fostering*, 24, 3, 48–55

McAuley, P and Kremer, J M D (1990) On the fringes of society: adults and children in a West Belfast community, *New Community*, 16, 2, 247–259

McCay, N and Sinclair, R (1999) *Mixed Needs: Children from Cross-Community Families in Public Care in Northern Ireland*. National Children's Bureau

McCole, P, Kelly, B and Sinclair, R (2003) *Change for the Future: Young People's Views on Anti-Sectarianism*. National Children's Bureau

McFarlane, W G (1979) Mixed Marriages in Ballycuan, Northern Ireland, *Journal of Comparative Family Studies*, 10, 2, 191–205

Morgan, V, Smyth, M, Robinson, G and Fraser G (1996), *Mixed Marriages in Northern Ireland*, Centre for the Study of Conflict, University of Ulster

Morrow, D and Wilson, D (1996) *Ways out of Conflict: Resources for Community Relations Work*. Corrymeela Press

Muldoon, O and Cairns, E Learning to cope: children, young people and war in Frydenburg, E ed. (1999) *Learning to cope*. Oxford University Press

Muldoon, O T and Trew, K (1995) Patterns of stress appraisal in eight to eleven year old Northern Irish children, *Children's Environments*, 12, 49–56

Muldoon, O T and Trew, K (2000) Children's experience and adjustment to political conflict in Northern Ireland, *Journal of Peace Psychology*, 6, 2, 157–176

Muldoon, O T, Trew, K and Kilpatrick, R (2000) The legacy of the troubles on the young people's psychological and social development and their school life, *Youth and Society*, 32, 1, 6–28

NICIE (Northern Ireland Council for Integrated Education) (1998) *The Anti-Bias Curriculum*. NICIE

NICIE (2002) *NICIE Annual Report 2001–2002*. NICIE

NIHE (Northern Ireland Housing Executive) (1999) *Towards a Community Relations Strategy*. Northern Ireland Housing Executive

Northern Ireland Statistics and Research Agency (1997) *Continuous Household Survey*

Northern Ireland Statistics and Research Agency (2003) *Census report 1. Demography; People, Family and Households*. TSO

Okitikpi, T (1999a) Mixed Race Children, *Social Work Education*, 19, 1

Okitikpi, T (1999b) Children of Mixed Parentage in Care: Why Such a High Number? *Child Care in Practice,* 5, 4, 396–405

Parker, R ,Ward, H, Jackson, S, Aldgate, J and Wedge, P eds (1991) Assessing Outcomes in Child Care. HMSO

Phoenix, A and Owen, C From Miscegenation to Hybridity: Mixed Relationships and Mixed-Parentage in Profile *in* Bernstein, B and Brannen, J eds (1996) *Children, Research and Policy.* Taylor and Francis

Pinkerton, J Social Work and the Troubles: New Opportunities for Engagement, pp15–29 *in* Central Council for Education and Training in Social Work CCETSW (1998) *Social Work and Social Change in Northern Ireland: Issues for Contemporary Practice* CCETSW (NI)

Pinkerton, J and Campbell, J (2002) Social Work and Social Justice in Northern Ireland: Towards a new occupational space, *British Journal of Social Work*, 32, 723–37

Playboard (1997) *Games not Names.* Playboard and Community Relations Council

Prevatt Goldstein, B *in* Barn, R ed. (1999) *Working with Black Children and Adolescents in Need.* BAAF

Robinson, G (1992) *Cross-Community Marriage in Northern Ireland.* Centre for Social Research, Queen's University Belfast

Root, M (1996) *The Multiracial Experience*. Sage

Rubin, H J and Rubin, I S (1995) *Qualitative Interviewing: The Art of Hearing Data*. Sage

Shirlow, P (1999) *Fear, Mobility and Living in the Ardoyne and Upper Ardoyne Communities.* School of Environmental Studies University of Ulster

Sinclair, R and Hai, N (2003) *Children of Dual Heritage in care in Islington*. National Children's Bureau

Social Services Inspectorate (NI) (1994) *Quality Living standards for services: Children who live away from home.* DHSS

Small, J M Transracial Placements: Conflicts and Contradictions *in* Ahmed, S, Cheetham, J, and Small, J eds (1986) *Social Work with Black Children and their Families*. BAAF

Smyth, M (1994) *Social Work, Sectarianism and Anti-Discriminatory Social Work Practice in Northern Ireland.* Department of Applied Social Studies, University of Ulster at Magee

Smyth, M (1998) *Half the Battle: Understanding the impact of the troubles on children and young people.* INCORE

Smyth, M and Campbell, J (1996*)* Social Work, Sectarianism and Anti-Sectarian Practice in Northern Ireland, *British Journal of Social Work*, 26, 1, 77–92.

Smyth, M and Robinson, G eds (2001) *Researching Violently Divided Societies: Ethical and Methodological Issues.* Pluto Press

Social Services Inspectorate (NI) (1995) *Quality Living standards for services: Children living in family placements*. DHSS

Spencer, J M (1997) *The New Coloured People: The Mixed Parentage People in America*. New York: University Press

Stalker, K (1998) Some Ethical and Methodological Issues in Research with People with Learning Difficulties. *Disability and Society*, 13, 1, 5–19

Stevens, H (2000) The Human Rights Act 1998: Implications for Children Child. *Care in Practice*, 6, 3, 264–268

Stringer, M and Cairns, E (1983) Catholic and Protestant young people's ratings of stereotype Catholic and Protestant faces, *British Journal of Social Psychology*, 22, 241–46

Thoburn, J (1994) *Child Placement: Principles and Practice*. Ashgate

Thompson, N (1993) *Anti-Discriminatory Practice*. Macmillan

Titterton, M (1995) Children's Rights to Legal Services: A Child Law Centre for Northern Ireland, *Child Care in Practice*, 1, 3, 47–53

Tizard, B and Phoenix, A (1993) *Black, White or Mixed Parentage*. Routledge

Traynor, C Social Work in a Sectarian Society *in* Central Council for Education and Training in Social Work CCETSW (1998) *Social Work and Social Change in Northern Ireland: Issues for Contemporary Practice*. CCETSW (NI)

Troyna, B and Hatcher, R (1992) *Racism in Children's Lives: A Study of Mainly-White Schools*. Routledge

Tunnard, J, Matching needs and services *in* Ward, H and Rose, W (2002) *Approaches to needs Assessment in Children's Services*. Jessica Kingsley

Wigfall-Williams, W W (2001) *Mixed Marriages: The International Dimension*. Conference Proceedings, 26–27 November 2001, Belfast

Wigfall-Williams, W W and Robinson, G (2001) A World Apart: Mixed Marriage in Northern Ireland. *Northern Ireland Life and Times Survey*, Research Update Number 8, November 2001

Wright, F Integrated education and political identity, pp182–194 *in* Moffatt, C ed. (1993) *Education together for a change*. Fortnight Educational Trust